*Food Engineering
Data Handbook*

General Editor: David Browning

Food Engineering Data Handbook

George D. Hayes

Senior Lecturer in Food Engineering
Department of Food Manufacture and Distribution

Manchester Polytechnic

Longman
Scientific &
Technical

Copublished in the United States with
John Wiley & Sons, Inc., New York

Longman Scientific and Technical
Longman Group UK Limited
Longman House, Burnt Mill, Harlow
Essex CM20 2JE, England
and Associated Companies throughout the world

Copublished in the United States with
John Wiley & Sons, Inc., 605 Third Avenue, New York, NY 10158

First published 1987

British Library Cataloguing in Publication Data
Hayes, George D.
  Food engineering data handbook.
  1. Food industry and trade
  I. Title
  664   TP370
  ISBN 0-582-49505-9

Library of Congress Cataloging in Publication Data
Hayes, George D., 1930–
  Food engineering data handbook.
  Includes index.
  1. Food industry and trade—Handbooks, manuals, etc.
I. Title
TP370.H39   1987   664′.00212   87-3992
ISBN 0-470-20840-6 (Wiley, USA only)

Printed in Great Britain at The Bath Press, Avon

Contents

CHAPTER 4 FOOD THERMAL DATA

CHAPTER 5 FOOD PROCESSING, STORAGE AND PACKAGING DATA

Preface

The compiler, in his food engineering and food plant design-studies over the past three decades, has been aware of the need for a compact and concise data-source containing the technical information relating to food engineering and to food science. Indeed, in the compiler's experience, countless hours have been wasted in the search for technical data relating to foods. Often, in those frantic searches for information, a 'guestimate' or 'ballpark' figure was all that was required for the particular food or engineering property.

The main aim of the manuscript is, therefore, to provide that data related to food manufacture, in a convenient and accessible form. However, because the food industries of the western world are developing so rapidly and span so wide a range, it is recognised that there will inevitably be some omissions. The compiler hopes that such omissions will not drastically reduce the value of the manuscript.

It was agreed from the start by all whose advice was sought that the success of this publication would depend upon its format and presentation. Accordingly, the manuscript has been divided into five chapters, with a more detailed list of chapter content preceding each chapter.

The first chapter is intended as an introductory section, and deals with the wide range of units used in food manufacture and conversion between them. It was considered prudent to confine all the 'non-food' data into a separate section under the heading Engineering Data; Chapter 2 therefore contains a good deal of the information that the food engineer is likely to need. The chemical and physical properties of foods are listed in Chapter 3, including data on food liquids, particulate solids and gases used in the food industry. Chapter 4 contains much of the thermal data relating to foods together with the formulae required to predict those properties and an associated computer program. All the data relating to food packaging and storage is included in the final chapter, including a glossary of canning terms, lists of recommended processing conditions and suggested recipes.

The compiler owes a great deal to the many scholars and industrial colleagues who have contributed to the manuscript. Sincere thanks are due in particular to David Browning who started the ball rolling; to Professor Alan Bailey and his team at the AFRC (Institute of Food Research, Bristol); to Metal Box plc; to Lyn Bates of Ajax Equipment Ltd; and finally to Tina Mason of Vuman Computer Systems Ltd who took upon the onerous task of typing the document.

G. D. Hayes
May 1987

1 Introduction

1.1   The international system of units.

    1.1.1   Prefixes.
    1.1.2   Definitions.

1.2   Other systems of units.

    1.2.1   Engineering system.
    1.2.2   Metric system.
    1.2.3   FPS system.

1.3   Examples of derived units and the symbols used.

1.4   Fundamental chemical and physical constants.

    1.4.1   List of elements and their atomic numbers.
    1.4.2   Physical constants.

1.5   Tables of common conversions.

    1.5.1   Alphabetical list of common conversions.
    1.5.2   Temperature conversions.
    1.5.3   Traditional degrees of sugar boiling.
    1.5.4   Reduced pressure. Approximate conversion
          tables.
    1.5.5   Comparison of various hydrometer scales.
    1.5.6   Relationship between degrees brix, refractive
          indexes, degrees baumé and specific gravity
          for sugar (sucrose) solutions.
    1.5.7   Relationship between salometer readings,
          specific gravity, degrees baumé and the
          concentration of brine solutions.
    1.5.8   Graph of percentage salt versus degrees
          twaddell for brine solutions.

1.6   Irradiation units.

    1.6.1   Radiation preservation - required dosages of
          radiation.

1.7   Vitamins - international units.

1.1 The International System of Units

This system is based upon the following seven fundamental units; metre (m); kilogram (kg); second (s); ampere (A); kelvin (K); candela (cd); mole (mol).

In addition the following supplementary or derived units are adopted:

Force = mass x acceleration

The SI unit of force is the newton (N), where

$$1 \text{ (N)} = 1 \text{ kg x } 1 \text{ m/s}^2 = 1 \text{ kg m/s}^2$$

The SI unit of work or energy is the joule (J) where 1 joule (J) = 1 Nm, since

1 joule (J) = 1 N x 1 m
1 joule (J) = 1 Nm

The SI unit of power is the watt (W) = 1 J/s since,

power = rate of doing work = J/s = watt

1.1.1 Prefixes

The following multiples and submultiples of each unit are adopted:

Factor	Prefix	Symbol	Factor	Prefix	Symbol
10^{18}	exa	E	10^{-1}	deci	d
10^{15}	peta	P	10^{-2}	centi	c
10^{12}	tera	T	10^{-3}	milli	m
10^{9}	giga	G	10^{-6}	micro	μ
10^{6}	mega	M	10^{-9}	nano	n
10^{3}	kilo	k	10^{-12}	pico	p
10^{2}	hecto	h	10^{-15}	femto	f
10^{1}	deca	da	10^{-18}	atto	a

1.1.2 Definitions

Quantity	Name	Symbol	Definition
Length	metre	m	1 650 763.73 wavelengths in vacuum of the radiation corresponding to the transition between the levels 2P and 5d, of the krypton - 86 atom.

Quantity	Name	Symbol	Definition
Time	second	s	Duration of 9 192 631 770 periods of the radiation corresponding to the transition between the two hyperfine levels at the ground state of the caesium 133 atom.
Mass	kilogram	kg	Mass of platinum-iridium prototype kept at the International Bureau of Weights and Measures. The kilogram is the only base unit defined by an artifact.
Electric current	ampere	A	That current that is maintained in two straight parallel conductors of infinite length, of negligible circular cross sections, and placed one metre apart in vacuum would produce between these conductors a force equal to 2×10^{-7} N per metre of length.
Temperature	kelvin	K	Used to express an interval or difference of temperature equal to the fraction $1/273.16$ of the thermodynamic temperature of the triple point of water.
Amount of substance	mole	mol	The amount of a substance of a system that contains as many elementary entities as there are atoms in 0.012 kg of carbon.
Luminous intensity	candela	cd	The luminous intensity of 1/600 000 of a square metre of a radiating cavity at the temperature of freezing platinum (2042 K).

1.2   Other Systems of Units

A number of other systems of units have been devised.   In particular the Engineering system enjoyed wide acceptance in the past.   Referring back to Newton's second law of motion:

Force = (factor of proportionality)(mass)(acceleration)

The use of this factor of proportionality depends only on the units adopted to measure force, but unfortunately since it has become traditional to represent this factor by the symbol 1/g, students tend to associate it with the acceleration due to gravity.

Newton's second law may be written:

$$F = 1/g \ Ma$$

so that when force is measured in newtons, mass in kilograms and length in metres:

$$1 \ N = 1/g \ (1 \ kg)(1 \ m/s^2)$$

then $g = 1 \ kg \ m/s^2$

1.2.1 Engineering System

In the Engineering system a pound mass is defined as a certain fraction (1/2.2046) of the standard kilogram, the unit of length is the foot, and the unit of time is the second.

In this Engineering system one pound–force (1 bf) will accelerate 1 lbm (one pound mass) at the rate of 32.174 ft/s².

$$1 \ lbf \ (F) = (\text{proportionality factor})(1 \ lbm)(32.174 \ ft/s^2)$$

$$1 \ lbf \quad = 1/g \ (1 \ lbm) \ (32.174 \ ft/s^2)$$

$$g \qquad = 32.174 \ \frac{ft \ 1lbm}{1 \ lbf \ s^2}$$

1.2.2 Metric System

In the Metric or Centimetre–gram–second (CGS) system the basic units are as follows; length = 1 centimetre; mass = 1 gram; time = 1 second.

The unit of force which will give a mass of 1 gram an acceleration of 1 cm/s² is known as the dyne.

1 dyne will accelerate 1 gram at a rate of 1 cm/s²

1.2.3 FPS System

In the FPS system the basic units are length = 1 foot; mass = 1 lb (1/2.2046 kilogram); time = 1 second.

The unit of force, the poundal, is that force which will impart an acceleration of 1 ft/s² to a mass of 1 pound.

1 poundal will accelerate 1 lbm at a rate of 1 ft/s².

1.3 Examples of Derived Units and the Symbols Used

Quantity	Symbol	Units
Acceleration	a	ms^{-2}
Angular velocity	ω	$rad\ s^{-1}$
Area	A	m^{-2}
Density	ρ	kgm^{-3}
Electrical capacitance	C	CV^{-1}
Electrical charge	Q	As^{-1}
Electrical potential	V	WA^{-1}
Electrical resistance	R	VA^{-1}
Energy	J	J
Enthalpy	H	J
Force	F	N
Frequency	f	s^{-1}
Heat flux	–	Wm^{-2}
Heat transfer coefficient	h	$Wm^{-2}K^{-1}$
Intensity of illuminations	–	cd
Luminous flux	–	cd sr
Mass transfer coefficient	Kg	$kgm^{-2}s^{-1}$
Mole fraction	M	
Mass flow rate	G	$kgm^{-2}s^{-1}$
Number	n	
Overall heat transfer coefficient	U	$Wm^{-2}K^{-1}$
Plane angle	θ	rad
Pressure	P	Nm^{-2}

continued over

Quantity	Symbol	Units
Power	P	Js^{-1}
Specific energy	E	Jkg^{-1}
Specific heat	c_p	$Jkg^{-1} K^{-1}$
Specific volume	V	$m^3 kg^{-1}$
Thermal diffusivity	α	$m^2 s^{-1}$
Thermal conductivity	λ	$Wm^{-1} K^{-1}$
Velocity	u	ms^{-1}
Viscosity absolute	μ	$Ns^{-1}m^{-1}m$
Viscosity kinematic	v	$m^2 s^{-1}$
Volume	V	m^3
Water content	W	kg^{-1}

1.4 Fundamental Chemical and Physical Constants

1.4.1 List of the Elements and their Atomic Numbers

Atomic number Z	Symbol	Name	Atomic number Z	Symbol	Name
1	H	Hydrogen	17	Cl	Chlorine
2	He	Helium	18	A	Argon
3	Li	Lithium	19	K	Potassium
4	Be	Beryllium	20	Ca	Calcium
5	B	Boron	21	Sc	Scadium
6	C	Carbon	22	Ti	Titanium
7	N	Nitrogen	23	V	Vanadium
8	O	Oxygen	24	Cr	Chromium
9	F	Fluorine	25	Mn	Manganese
10	Ne	Neon	26	Fe	Iron
11	Na	Sodium	27	Co	Cobalt
12	Mg	Magnesium	28	Ni	Nickel
13	Al	Aluminium	29	Cu	Copper
14	Si	Silicon	30	Zn	Zinc
15	P	Phosphorus	31	Ga	Gallium
16	S	Sulphur	32	Ge	Germanium

Atomic number Z	Symbol	Name	Atomic number Z	Symbol	Name
33	As	Arsenic	70	Yb	Ytterbium
34	Se	Selenium	71	Lu	Luttetium
35	Br	Bromine	72	Hf	Hafnium
36	Kr	Krypton	73	Ta	Tantalum
37	Rb	Rubidium	74	W	Tungsten
38	Sr	Strontium	75	Re	Rhenium
39	Y	Yttrium	76	Os	Osmium
40	Zr	Zirconium	77	Ir	Iridium
41	Nb	Niobium	78	Pt	Platinum
42	Mo	Molybdenum	79	Au	Gold
43	Tc	*Technetium*	80	Hg	Mercury
44	Ru	Ruthenium	81	Tl	Thallium
45	Rh	Rhodium	82	Pb	Lead
46	Pd	Palladium	83	Bi	Bismuth
47	Ag	Silver	84	Po	Polonium
48	Cd	Cadmium	85	At	*Astatine*
49	In	Indium	86	Rn	Radon
50	Sn	Tin	87	Fr	*Francium*
51	Sb	Antimony	88	Ra	Radium
52	Te	Tellurium	89	Ac	Actinium
53	I	Iodine	90	Th	Thorium
54	Xe	Xenon	91	Pa	Protactinium
55	Cs	Caesium	92	U	Uranium
56	Ba	Barium	93	Np	*Neptunium*
57	La	Lanthium	94	Pu	*Plutonium*
58	Ce	Cerium	95	Am	*Americium*
59	Pr	Praseodymium	96	Cm	*Curium*
60	Nd	Neodymium	97	Bk	*Berkelium*
61	Pm	Promethium	98	Cf	*Californium*
62	Sm	Samarium	99	E	*Einsteinium*
63	Eu	Europium	100	Fm	*Fermium*
64	Gd	Gadolinium	101	Mv	*Mendelevium*
65	Tb	Terbium	102	No	*Nobelium*
66	Dy	Dysprosium	103	Lw	*Lawrencium*
67	Ho	Holmium	104	Ku	*Kurchatovium*
68	Er	Erbium	105	Ha	*Hahnium*
69	Tm	Thulium			

The elements printed in italic do not occur naturally, but have been produced artificially.

1.4.2   Physical Constants

(i)   The basis of natural logarithms e = 2.7183

(ii)   Gravitational acceleration g = 9.80665 m/s^2

(iii) Pi Π = 3.1416

(iv)   Plank's Constant h = 6.626 x 10^{-34}Js

(v)   Speed of light c = 3 x 10^8 m/s

(vi)   Universal Gas Constant

                                             R = 8.314 J/mol.K

1.5   Tables of Common Conversions

1.5.1   Alphabetical List of Common Conversions

Acceleration	1 cm/s^2	:	1.000 0 x 10^{-2} m/s^2
	1 m/h^2	:	7.716 0 x 10^{-3} m/s^2
	1 ft/s^2	:	3.048 0 x 10^{-1} m/s^2
Area	1 cm^2	:	1.000 0 x 10^{-4} m^2
	1 ft^2	:	9.290 3 x 10^{-2} m^2
	1 in^2	:	6.451 6 x 10^{-4} m^2
	1 yd^2	:	8.361 3 x 10^{-2} m^2
	1 acre	:	4.046 9 x 10^3 m^2
	1 mile^2	:	2.590 0 x 10^4 m^2
Calorific Value	1 cal/cm^3	:	4.186 8 x 10^6 J/m^3
	1 kcal/m^3	:	4.186 8 x 10^3 J/m^3
	1 Btu/ft^3	:	3.726 0 x 10^4 J/m^3
	1 Chu/ft^3	:	6.706 7 x 10^4 J/m^3
	1 therm/ft^3	:	3.726 0 x 10^9 J/m^3
	1 kcal/ft^3	:	1.478 6 x 10^5 J/m^3
Coefficient of Expansion (volumetric)	1 g/cm^3 ^{o}C	:	1.000 0 x 10^3 ^{o}C
	1 lb/ft^3 ^{o}F	:	2.883 3 x 10 kg/m^3 ^{o}C
	1 lb/ft^3 ^{o}C	:	1.601 8 x 10 kg/m^3 ^{o}C
Density	1 g/cm^3	:	1.000 0 x 10^3 kg/m^3
	1 lb/ft^3	:	1.601 8 x 10 kg/m^3
	1 lb/UK gal	:	9.977 9 x 10 kg/m^3
	1 lb/US gal	:	1.198 3 x 10^2 kg/m^3
	1 kg/ft^3	:	3.531 5 x 10 kg/m^3

Energy	1 cal	:	$4.186\ 8$ J
	1 kcal	:	$4.186\ 8 \times 10^3$ J
	1 Btu	:	$1.055\ 1 \times 10^3$ J
	1 erg	:	$1.000\ 0 \times 10^{-7}$ J
	1 hp h(metric)	:	$2.647\ 7 \times 10^6$ J
	1 kW h	:	$3.600\ 0 \times 10^6$ J
	1 ft pdl	:	$4.213\ 9 \times 10^{-2}$ J
	1 ft lbf	:	$1.355\ 8$ J
	1 Chu	:	$1.899\ 1 \times 10^3$ J
	1 hph(Imp)	:	$2.684\ 5 \times 10^6$ J
	1 therm	:	$1.055\ 1 \times 10^2$ J
	1 thermie	:	$4.185\ 5 \times 10^6$ J
	1 ft kgf	:	$2.989\ 1$ J
Force	1 dyn	:	$1.000\ 0 \times 10^{-5}$ N
	1 kgf	:	$9.806\ 7$ N
	1 pdl	:	$1.382\ 5 \times 10^{-1}$ N
	1 lbf	:	$4.448\ 2$ N
	1 tonf	:	9.964×10^3 N
Heat flux	1 cal/s cm^2	:	$4.186\ 8 \times 10^4$ W/m^2
	1 kcal/h m^2	:	$1.163\ 0$ W/m^2
	1 Btu/h ft^2	:	$3.154\ 6$ W/m^2
	1 Chu/h ft^2	:	$5.678\ 4$ W/m^2
	1 kcal/h ft^2	:	$1.251\ 8$ W/m^2
Heat release (mass)	1 cal/s g	:	$4.186\ 8 \times 10^3$ W/kg
	1 kcal/h kg	:	$1.163\ 0$ W/kg
	1 Btu/h lb	:	$6.461\ 2 \times 10^{-2}$ W/kg
Heat release rate (volumetric)	1 cal/s cm^3	:	$4.186\ 8 \times 10^6$ W/m^3
	1 kcal/h m^3	:	$1.163\ 0$ W/m^3
	1 Btu/h ft^3	:	$1.035\ 0 \times 10$ W/m^3
	1 Chu/h ft^3	:	$1.863\ 0 \times 10$ W/m^3
Heat transfer coefficient	1 cal/s cm^2 ^{0}C	:	$4.186\ 8 \times 10^6$ W/m^2 K
Length	1 cm	:	$1.000\ 0 \times 10^{-3}$ m
	1 ft	:	$3.048\ 0 \times 10^{-1}$ m
	1 Angstrom	:	$1.000\ 0 \times 10^{-10}$ m
	1 micron	:	$1.000\ 0 \times 10^{-6}$ m
	1 in	:	$2.540\ 0 \times 10^{-2}$ m
	1 yd	:	$9.144\ 0 \times 10^{-1}$ m
	1 mile	:	$1.609\ 3 \times 10^3$ m
Mass	1 g	:	$1.000\ 0 \times 10^{-3}$ kg
	1 lb	:	$4.535\ 9 \times 10^{-1}$ kg
	1 tonne	:	$1.000\ 0 \times 10^3$ kg
	1 grain	:	$6.480\ 0 \times 10^{-5}$ kg
	1 oz	:	$2.835\ 0 \times 10^{-3}$ kg
	1 cwt	:	$5.080\ 2 \times 10$ kg
	1 ton	:	$1.016\ 0 \times 10^3$ kg

continued over

Mass per unit area	1 g/cm^2	:	$1.000\ 0 \times 10$ kg/m^2
	1 lb/ft^2	:	$4.883\ 4$ kg/m^2
	1 lb/in^2	:	$7.030\ 7 \times 10^2$ kg/m^2
	1 tonne/mile^2	:	$3.923\ 0 \times 10^{-4}$ kg/m^2
	1 kg/ft^2	:	$1.076\ 4 \times 10$ kg/m^2
Mass flow	1 g/s	:	$1.000\ 0 \times 10^{-3}$ kg/s
	1 kg/h	:	$2.777\ 8 \times 10^{-4}$ kg/s
	1 lb/s	:	$4.535\ 9 \times 10^{-4}$ kg/s
	1 tonne/h	:	$2.777\ 8 \times 10^{-3}$ kg/s
	1 lb/h	:	$1.260\ 0 \times 10^{-4}$ kg/s
	1 ton/h	:	$2.822\ 4 \times 10^{-3}$ kg/s
Mass flux	1 g/s cm^2	:	$1.000\ 0 \times 10$ kg/s m^2
	1 kg/h m^2	:	$2.777\ 8 \times 10^{-6}$ kg/s m^2
	1 lb/s ft^2	:	$4.882\ 4$ kg/s m^2
	1 lb/h ft^2	:	$1.356\ 2 \times 10^{-3}$ kg/s m$_2$
	1 kg/h ft^2	:	$2.990\ 0 \times 10^{-3}$ kg/s m^2
Mass release rate	1 g/s cm^3	:	$1.000\ 0 \times 10^3$ kg/s m^3
	1 kg/h m^3	:	$2.777\ 8 \times 10^{-5}$ kg/s m^3
	1 lb/s ft^3	:	$1.601\ 8 \times 10$ kg/s m^3
	1 lb/h ft^3	:	$4.449\ 6 \times 10^{-3}$ kg/s m^3
	1 kg/h ft^3	:	$9.899\ 6 \times 10^{-3}$ kg/s m^3
Mass transfer coefficient	1 g/s cm^{2}atm	:	$9.868\ 7 \times 10^{-5}$ N/m^2
	1 kg/h m^{2}atm	:	$2.741\ 3 \times 10^{-9}$ N/m^2
	1 lb/h ft^{2}atm	:	$1.338\ 4 \times 10^{-6}$ N/m^2
	1 kg/h ft^{2}atm	:	$2.959\ 7 \times 10^{-3}$ N/m^2
Momentum, angular	1 g cm^2/s	:	$1.000\ 0 \times 10^{-2}$ kg m^2/s
	1 lb ft^2/s	:	$4.214\ 0 \times 10^{-2}$ kg m^2/s
	1 lb ft^2/h	:	$1.170\ 6 \times 10^{-6}$ kg m^2/s
Momentum, linear	1 g cm/s	:	$1.000\ 0 \times 10^{-6}$ kg m/s
	1 lb ft/s	:	$1.382\ 5 \times 10^{-3}$ kg m/s
	1 lb ft/h	:	$3.840\ 4 \times 10^{-2}$ kg m/s
Moment of inertia	1 g cm^2	:	$1.000\ 0 \times 10^{-7}$ kg m^2
	1 lb ft^2	:	$4.214\ 0 \times 10^{-2}$ kg m^2
Power	1 cal/s	:	$4.186\ 8$ W
	1 kcal/h	:	$1.163\ 0$ W
	1 Btu/s	:	$1.055\ 1 \times 10^3$ W
	1 erg/s	:	$1.000\ 0 \times 10^7$ W
	1 tonne cal/h	:	$1.163\ 0 \times 10^3$ W
	1 hp (metric)	:	$7.354\ 8 \times 10^2$ W
	1 ft pdl/s	:	$4.213\ 9 \times 10^{-2}$ W
	1 ft lbf/s	:	$1.355\ 8$ W
	1 Btu/h	:	$2.930\ 8 \times 10^{-1}$ W
	1 Chu/h	:	$5.275\ 4 \times 10^{-1}$ W
	1 hp (British)	:	$7.457\ 0 \times 10^2$ W
	1 ton (refrigeration)	:	$3.516\ 9 \times 10^3$ W

Pressure	1 dyn/cm^2	:	$1.000\ 0 \times 10^{-1}$ N/m^2
	1 kgf/m^2	:	$9.806\ 7$ N/m^2
	1 pdl/ft^2	:	$1.488\ 1$ N/m^2
	1 std atmos	:	$1.013\ 3 \times 10^5$ N/m^2
	1 atmos	:	$9.806\ 7 \times 10^4$ N/m^2
	1 bar	:	$1.000\ 0 \times 10^5$ N/m^2
	1 lbf/ft^2	:	$4.788\ 0 \times 10$ N/m^2
	1 tonf/in^2	:	$1.544\ 4 \times 10^7$ N/m^2
	1 in water	:	$2.490\ 9 \times 10^2$ N/m^2
	1 ft water	:	$2.989\ 1 \times 10^3$ N/m^2
	1 mm Hg	:	$1.333\ 3 \times 10^2$ N/m^2
	1 in Hg	:	$3.386\ 6 \times 10^3$ N/m^2
Specific enthalpy	1 cal/g	:	$4.186\ 8 \times 10^3$ J/kg
	1 Btu/lb	:	$2.326\ 0 \times 10^3$ J/kg
	1 Chu/lb	:	$4.186\ 8 \times 10^3$ J/kg
Specific heat	1 cal/g ^{0}C	:	$4.186\ 8 \times 10^3$ J/kg ^{0}C
	1 Btu/lb ^{0}F	:	$4.186\ 8 \times 10^3$ J/kg ^{0}C
Specific volume	1 cm^3/g	:	$1.000\ 0 \times 10^{-3}$ m^3/kg
	1 ft^3/lb	:	$6.242\ 8 \times 10^{-2}$ m^3/kg
	1 ft^3/kg	:	$2.831\ 7 \times 10^{-2}$ m^3/kg
Surface per unit mass	1 cm^2/g	:	$1.000\ 0 \times 10^{-1}$ m^2/kg
	1 ft^2/lb	:	$2.048\ 2 \times 10^{-1}$ m^2/kg
	1 m^2/g	:	$1.000\ 0 \times 10^3$ m^2/kg
	1 ft^2/kg	:	$9.290\ 3 \times 10^{-2}$ m^2/kg
Surface per unit volume	1 cm^2/cm^3	:	$1.000\ 0 \times 10^2$ m^2/m^3
	1 ft^2/ft^3	:	$3.280\ 8$ m^2/m^3
Surface tension	1 dyn/cm	:	1.000×10^{-3} N/m
Temperature difference	1 deg F (^{0}R)	:	5/9 deg C (K)
Thermal conductivity	1 cal/s cm^2	:	$4.186\ 8 \times 10^2$ W/m^2
	1 kcal/h m^2	:	$1.163\ 0$ W/m^2
	1 Btu/h ft^2	:	$1.730\ 8$ W/m^2
	1 Btu/h ft^2(^{0}F/in)	:	$1.412\ 3 \times 10^{-1}$ W/m^2
	1 kcal/h ft^2	:	$3.815\ 6$ W/m^2
Time	1 h	:	$3.600\ 0 \times 10^3$ s
	1 min	:	$6.000\ 0 \times 10$ s
	1 day	:	$8.640\ 0 \times 10^4$ s
	1 year	:	$3.155\ 8 \times 10^7$ s
Velocity	1 cm/s	:	$1.000\ 0 \times 10^{-2}$ m/s
	1 m/h	:	$2.777\ 8 \times 10^{-4}$ m/s
	1 ft/s	:	$3.048\ 0 \times 10^{-1}$ m/s
	1 ft/h	:	$8.466\ 7 \times 10^{-5}$ m/s
	1 mile/h	:	$4.470\ 4 \times 10^{-1}$ m/s

continued over

Viscosity (absolute)	1 g/cm s	:	$1.000\ 0 \times 10^{-1}$ N s/m^2
	1 kg/m h	:	$2.777\ 8 \times 10^{-4}$ kg/ms
	1 lb/ft s	:	$1.488\ 2$ kg/m s
	1 lb/ft h	:	$4.133\ 8 \times 10^{-4}$ kg/ms
	1 kg/ft h	:	$9.113\ 4 \times 10^{-4}$ kg/ms
Viscosity (kinematic)	1 cm^2/s	:	$1.000\ 0 \times 10^{-4}$ m^2/s
	1 m^2/h	:	$2.777\ 8 \times 10^{-4}$ m^2/s
	1 ft^2/s	:	$9.290\ 3 \times 10^{-2}$ m^2/s
	1 ft^2/h	:	$2.580\ 6 \times 10^{-5}$ m^2/s
Volume	1 cm^3	:	$1.000\ 0 \times 10^{-6}$ m^3
	1 ft^3	:	$2.831\ 7 \times 10^{-2}$ m^3
	1 litre	:	$1.000\ 0 \times 10^{-3}$ m^3
	1 in^3	:	$1.638\ 7 \times 10^{-5}$ m^3
	1 yd^3	:	$7.645\ 5 \times 10^{-1}$ m^3
	1 UK gal	:	$4.546\ 0 \times 10^{-3}$ m^3
	1 US gal	:	$3.785\ 3 \times 10^{-3}$ m^3
Volumetric flow	1 cm^3/s	:	$1.000\ 0 \times 10^{-6}$ m^3/s
	1 m^3/h	:	$2.777\ 8 \times 10^{-4}$ m^3/s
	1 ft^3/s	:	$2.831\ 7 \times 10^{-2}$ m^3/s
	1 cm^3/min	:	$1.666\ 7 \times 10^{-3}$ m^3/s
	1 litre/min	:	$1.666\ 7 \times 10^{-5}$ m^3/s
	1 ft^3/min	:	$4.719\ 5 \times 10^{-4}$ m^3/s
	1 ft^3/h	:	$7.865\ 8 \times 10^{-6}$ m^3/s
	1 UK gal/min	:	$7.576\ 6 \times 10^{-5}$ m^3/s
	1 US gal/min	:	$6.308\ 9 \times 10^{-5}$ m^3/s
	1 UK gal/h	:	$1.262\ 8 \times 10^{-6}$ m^3/s
	1 US gal/h	:	$1.051\ 5 \times 10^{-6}$ m^3/s
Wetting rate (volumetric)	1 litre/h in	:	$1.093\ 6 \times 10^{-5}$ m^3/s m

1.5.2   Temperature Conversions

°C		°F	°C		°F
-273.1	-459.4	–	-17.2	1	33.8
-268	-450	–	-16.7	2	35.8
-262	-440	–	-16.1	3	37.4
-257	-430	–	-15.6	4	39.2
-251	-420	–	-15	5	41
-246	-410	–	-14.4	6	42.8
-240	-400	–	-13.9	7	44.6
-234	-390	–	-13.3	8	46.4
-229	-380	–	-12.8	9	48.2
-223	-370	–	-12.2	10	50
-218	-360	–	-11.7	11	51.8
-212	-350	–	-11.1	12	53.6
-207	-340	–	-10.6	13	55.4
-201	-330	–	-10	14	57.2
-196	-320	–	-9.44	15	59
-190	-310	–	-9.89	16	60.8
-184	-300	–	-8.33	17	62.6
-179	-290	–	-7.78	18	64.4
-173	-280	–	-7.22	19	66.2
-169	-273	-459.4	-6.67	20	68
-168	-270	-454	-6.11	21	69.8
-162	-260	-436	-5.56	22	71.6
-157	-250	-418	-5	23	73.4
-151	-240	-400	-4.44	24	75.2
-146	-230	-382	-3.89	25	77
-140	-220	-364	-3.33	26	78.88
-134	-210	-346	-2.78	27	80.6
-129	-200	-328	-2.22	28	82.4
-123	-190	-310	-1.67	29	84.2
-118	-180	-292	-1.11	30	86
-112	-170	-274	-0.56	31	87.8
-107	-160	-256	0	32	89.6
-101	-150	-238	0.56	33	91.4
-95.6	-140	-220	1.11	34	93.2
-90	-130	-202	1.67	35	95
-84.4	-120	-184	2.22	36	96.8
-78.9	-110	-166	2.78	37	98.6
-73.3	-100	-148	3.33	38	100.4
-67.8	-90	-130	3.89	39	102.2
-62.2	-80	-112	4.44	40	104
-56.7	-70	-94	5	41	105.8
-51.1	-60	-76	5.56	42	107.6
-45.6	-50	-58	6.11	43	109.4
-40	-40	-40	6.67	44	111.2
-34.4	-30	-22	7.22	45	113
-28.9	-20	-4	7.78	46	114.8
-23.3	-10	14	8.33	47	116.6
-17.8	0	32	8.89	48	118.4

continued over

°C		°F	°C		°F
9.44	49	120.2	66	150	302
10	50	122	71	160	320
10.6	51	123.8	77	170	338
11.1	52	125.6	82	180	356
11.7	53	127.4	88	190	374
12.2	54	129.2	93	200	392
12.8	55	131	99	210	410
13.3	56	132.8	100	212	413
13.9	57	134.6	104	220	428
14.4	58	136.4	110	230	446
15	59	138.2	116	240	464
15.6	60	140	121	250	482
16.1	61	141.8	127	260	500
16.7	62	143.6	132	270	518
17.2	63	145.4	138	280	536
17.8	64	147.2	149	300	572
18.3	65	149	154	310	590
18.9	66	150.8	160	320	608
19.4	67	152.6	166	330	626
20	68	154.4	171	340	644
20.6	69	156.2	177	350	662
21.1	70	158	182	360	680
23.9	75	167	188	370	698
26.7	80	176	193	380	716
29.4	85	185	199	390	734
32.2	90	194	204	400	752
35	95	203.3	210	410	770
35.6	96	204.8	216	420	788
36.1	97	206.6	221	430	806
36.7	98	208.4	227	440	824
37.2	99	210.2	232	450	842
37.8	100	212	238	460	824
43	109	230	243	470	878
49	120	248	249	480	896
54	130	266	254	490	914
60	140	284	260	500	932

Interpolation

°C		°F
0.56	1	1.8
1.11	2	3.6
1.67	3	5.4
2.22	4	7.2
2.78	5	9.0
3.33	6	10.8
3.89	7	12.6
4.44	8	14.4
5.00	9	16.2

1.5.3 Traditional Degrees of Sugar Boiling

Name	Test	Observation	Temperature °C	°F
Thread (gloss)	A	Thin strands	103	215
Large thread (large gloss)	A	Stronger and more strands	104	219
Small pearl	B	Forms small droplets	105	220
Large pearl	B	Forms large droplets	106	222
Blow (souffle)	C	Bubbles set on syrup	110	230
Feather	B	Forms feathery hard strands	111	232
Small ball	B	Syrup forms soft ball	116	240
Large ball	B	Syrup forms hard ball	120	248
Light crack	B	Forms thin sheet	129	264
Medium crack	B	Sheet forms, slightly brittle	133	271
Hard crack	B	Rapidly formed sheet	143	289
Extra hard crack	B	Sheet shows signs of browning	168	334
Caramel	B	Brown brittle sheet forms	180	356

Details of tests

Test A   Place sample of cooked syrup between two wetted fingers and open.

Test B   Dip finger or spatula (above 110 °C) in water, then in portion of boil, return to cold water.

Test C   Blow on spatula dipped in syrup.

1.5.4   Reduced Pressure – Approximate Conversion Table

Inches Mercury		mm Hg (torr)	lb/in^2 abs.	In Water abs.
Absolute	Vacuum Gauge			
29	1	735	14.2	394
28	2	709	13.7	381
27	3	684	13.2	367
26	4	659	12.7	354
25	5	633	12.2	340
24	6	608	11.8	326
23	7	583	11.3	313
22	8	557	10.8	299
21	9	532	10.3	286
20	10	507	9.8	272
19	11	481	9.3	258
18	12	456	8.8	245
17	13	431	8.3	231
16	14	405	7.8	218
15	15	380	7.3	204
14	16	355	6.9	190
13	17	329	6.4	177
12	18	304	5.9	163
11	19	279	5.4	150
10	20	253	4.9	136
9	21	228	4.4	122
8	22	203	3.9	109
7	23	177	3.4	95
6	24	152	2.9	82
5	25	127	2.4	68
4	26	101	2.0	54
3	27	76	1.5	41
2	28	51	1.0	27
1	29	25	0.49	14
0.8	29.2	20	0.39	11
0.6	29.4	15	0.29	8
0.4	29.6	10	0.20	5
0.2	29.8	5	0.10	3

Degrees Baumé	Specific Gravity	Degrees Twaddel 60°F	Degrees Brix 15.6°C
0	1.000	0	0
1	1.007	1.4	2.8
2	1.014	2.8	5.5
3	1.021	4.2	8.2
4	1.028	5.6	10.9
5	1.036	7.2	13.9
6	1.043	8.6	16.5
7	1.051	10.2	19.4
8	1.058	11.6	21.9
9	1.066	13.2	24.8
10	1.074	14.8	27.5
11	1.082	16.4	30.3
12	1.090	18.0	33.0
13	1.098	19.6	36.0
14	1.107	21.4	39.0
15	1.115	23.0	41.3
16	1.124	24.8	44.2
17	1.133	26.6	46.5
18	1.142	28.4	49.7
19	1.151	30.2	52.5
20	1.160	32.0	55.2
22	1.179	35.8	60.7
24	1.198	39.4	66.1
26	1.218	43.6	71.6
28	1.239	47.8	77.2
30	1.261	52.2	82.8
32	1.283	56.6	88.3
34	1.306	61.2	93.7
36	1.330	66.0	99.2
38	1.355	71.0	104.7
40	1.381	76.2	110.3
42	1.408	81.6	115.9
44	1.436	87.0	121.3
46	1.465	93.0	126.7
48	1.495	99.0	132.4
50	1.526	105.2	137.9
52	1.559	111.8	143.4
54	1.593	118.6	148.9
56	1.629	125.8	154.5
58	1.666	133.4	160.0
60	1.706	141.2	165.5
62	1.747	149.4	171.0
64	1.790	158.0	176.5
66	1.835	167.0	182.0
68	1.883	176.6	187.5
70	1.933	186.6	193.0
72.5	2.000	200.0	200.0

Relationship Between Degrees Brix, Degrees Baumé, Refractive Index (RI), and Specific Gravity (Sp Gr) of Sugar (Sucrose) Solutions

Degrees Brix	RI at 20°C	Degrees Baumé	Sp Gr 20°/20C	Degrees Brix	RI at 20°C	Degrees Baumé	Sp Gr 20°/20C
0.0	1.3330	0.00	1.0000	9.4	1.3469	5.24	1.0376
0.2	1.3333	0.11	1.0008	9.6	1.3472	5.35	1.0384
0.4	1.3336	0.22	1.0016	9.8	1.3475	5.46	1.0392
0.6	1.3339	0.34	1.0023	10.0	1.3478	5.57	1.0400
0.8	1.3341	0.45	1.0031	10.2	1.3481	5.68	1.0408
1.0	1.3344	0.56	1.0039	10.4	1.3485	5.80	1.0416
1.2	1.3347	0.67	1.0047	10.6	1.3488	5.91	1.0425
1.4	1.3350	0.79	1.0055	10.8	1.3491	6.02	1.0433
1.6	1.3353	0.90	1.0062	11.0	1.3494	6.13	1.0441
1.8	1.3356	1.01	1.0070	11.2	1.3497	6.24	1.0450
2.0	1.3359	1.12	1.0078	11.4	1.3500	6.35	1.0458
2.2	1.3362	1.23	1.0086	11.6	1.3503	6.46	1.0466
2.4	1.3365	1.34	1.0094	11.8	1.3506	6.57	1.0475
2.6	1.3368	1.46	1.0102	12.0	1.3509	6.68	1.0483
2.8	1.3370	1.57	1.0109	12.2	1.3512	6.79	1.0492
3.0	1.3373	1.68	1.0117	12.4	1.3516	6.90	1.0500
3.2	1.3376	1.79	1.0125	12.6	1.3519	7.02	1.0508
3.4	1.3379	1.90	1.0133	12.8	1.3519	7.13	1.0517
3.6	1.3382	2.02	1.0141	13.0	1.3525	7.24	1.0525
3.8	1.3385	2.13	1.0149	13.2	1.3528	7.35	1.0534
4.0	1.3388	2.24	1.0157	13.4	1.3531	7.46	1.0542
4.2	1.3391	2.35	1.0165	13.6	1.3534	7.57	1.0551
4.4	1.3394	2.46	1.0173	13.8	1.3538	7.68	1.0559
4.6	1.3397	2.57	1.0181	14.0	1.3541	7.79	1.0568
4.8	1.3400	2.68	1.0189	14.2	1.3544	7.90	1.0576
5.0	1.3403	2.79	1.0197	14.4	1.3547	8.01	1.0585
5.2	1.3406	2.91	1.0205	14.6	1.3550	8.12	1.0593
5.4	1.3409	3.02	1.0213	14.8	1.3554	8.23	1.0602
5.6	1.3412	3.13	1.0221	15.0	1.3557	8.34	1.0610
5.8	1.3415	3.24	1.0229	15.2	1.3560	8.45	1.0619
6.0	1.3418	3.35	1.0237	15.4	1.3563	8.56	1.0628
6.2	1.3421	3.46	1.0245	15.6	1.3566	8.67	1.0636
6.4	1.3424	3.57	1.0253	15.8	1.3570	8.78	1.0645
6.6	1.3427	3.69	1.0261	16.0	1.3573	8.89	1.0653
6.8	1.3430	3.80	1.0269	16.2	1.3576	9.00	1.0662
7.0	1.3433	3.91	1.0277	16.4	1.3579	9.11	1.0671
7.2	1.3436	4.02	1.0285	16.6	1.3563	8.56	1.0628
7.4	1.3439	4.13	1.0294	15.6	1.3566	8.67	1.0636
7.6	1.3442	4.24	1.0302	15.8	1.3570	8.78	1.0645
7.8	1.3445	4.35	1.0310	16.0	1.3573	8.89	1.0653
8.0	1.3448	4.46	1.0318	16.2	1.3576	9.00	1.0662
8.2	1.3451	4.58	1.0326	16.4	1.3579	9.11	1.0671
8.4	1.3454	4.69	1.0334	16.6	1.3582	9.22	1.0679
8.6	1.3457	4.80	1.0343	16.8	1.3586	9.33	1.0688
8.8	1.3460	4.91	1.0351	17.0	1.3589	9.45	1.0697
9.0	1.3463	5.02	1.0359	17.2	1.3592	9.56	1.0706
9.2	1.3466	5.13	1.0367	17.4	1.3596	9.67	1.0714

Degrees Brix	RI at 20°C	Degrees Baumé	Sp Gr 20°/20C	Degrees Brix	RI at 20°C	Degrees Baumé	Sp Gr 20°/20C
17.6	1.3599	9.78	1.0723	27.0	1.3758	14.93	1.1148
17.8	1.3602	9.89	1.0732	27.2	1.3761	15.04	1.1157
18.0	1.3605	10.00	1.0740	27.4	1.3765	15.15	1.1167
18.2	1.3609	10.11	1.0749	27.6	1.3768	15.26	1.1176
18.4	1.3612	10.22	1.0758	27.8	1.3772	15.37	1.1186
18.6	1.3615	10.33	1.0767	28.0	1.3775	15.48	1.1195
18.8	1.3618	10.44	1.0776	28.2	1.3779	15.59	1.1204
19.0	1.3622	10.55	1.0784	28.4	1.3782	15.69	1.1214
19.2	1.3625	10.66	1.0793	28.6	1.3786	15.80	1.1223
19.4	1.3628	10.77	1.0802	28.8	1.3789	15.91	1.1233
19.6	1.3632	10.88	1.0811	29.0	1.3793	16.02	1.1242
19.8	1.3635	10.99	1.0820	29.2	1.3797	16.13	1.1252
20.0	1.3638	11.10	1.0829	29.4	1.3800	16.24	1.1261
20.2	1.3642	11.21	1.0838	29.6	1.3804	16.35	1.1271
20.4	1.3645	11.32	1.0847	29.8	1.3807	16.46	1.1280
20.6	1.3648	11.43	1.0855	30.0	1.3811	16.57	1.1290
20.8	1.3652	11.54	1.0864	30.2	1.3815	16.67	1.1299
21.0	1.3655	11.65	1.0873	30.4	1.3818	16.78	1.1309
21.2	1.3658	11.76	1.0882	30.6	1.3822	16.89	1.1319
21.4	1.3662	11.87	1.0891	30.8	1.3825	17.00	1.1328
21.6	1.3665	11.98	1.0903	31.0	1.3829	17.11	1.1338
21.8	1.3668	12.09	1.0909	31.2	1.3833	17.22	1.1347
22.0	1.3672	12.20	1.0918	31.4	1.3836	17.33	1.1357
22.2	1.3675	12.31	1.0927	31.6	1.3840	17.43	1.1367
22.4	1.3679	12.42	1.0936	31.8	1.3843	17.54	1.1376
22.6	1.3682	12.52	1.0945	32.0	1.3847	17.65	1.1386
22.8	1.3685	12.63	1.0955	32.2	1.3851	17.76	1.1396
23.0	1.3689	12.74	1.0964	32.4	1.3854	17.87	1.1406
23.2	1.3692	12.85	1.0973	32.6	1.3858	17.98	1.1415
23.4	1.3696	12.96	1.0982	32.8	1.3861	18.08	1.1425
23.6	1.3699	13.07	1.0991	33.0	1.3865	18.19	1.1435
23.8	1.3703	13.18	1.1000	33.2	1.3869	18.30	1.1445
24.0	1.3706	13.29	1.1009	33.4	1.3872	18.41	1.1454
24.2	1.3709	13.40	1.1018	33.6	1.3876	18.52	1.1464
24.4	1.3713	13.51	1.1028	33.8	1.3879	18.63	1.1474
24.6	1.3716	13.62	1.1037	35.0	1.3902	19.28	1.1533
24.8	1.3720	13.73	1.1046	40.0	1.3997	21.97	1.1785
25.0	1.3723	13.84	1.1055	45.0	1.4096	24.63	1.2047
25.2	1.3726	13.95	1.1064	50.0	1.4200	27.28	1.2317
25.4	1.3730	14.06	1.1074	55.0	1.4307	28.54	1.2451
25.6	1.3733	14.17	1.1083	60.0	1.4418	32.49	1.2887
25.8	1.3737	14.28	1.1092	65.0	1.4532	35.04	1.3187
26.0	1.3740	14.39	1.1101	70.0	1.4651	37.56	1.3496
26.2	1.3744	14.49	1.1111	75.0	1.4774	40.03	1.3814
26.4	1.3747	14.60	1.1120	80.0	1.4901	42.47	1.4142
26.6	1.3751	14.71	1.1129	85.0	1.5033	44.86	1.4479
26.8	1.3754	14.82	1.1139				

1.5.7 Relationship Between Salometer Readings, Specific Gravity (SG), Degrees Baumé, and the Concentration of Brine Solutions

Salometer°	SG	Baumé°	Wt% NaCl	lb/gal Brine		lb Salt/ gal water	Freezing Point °F
				NaCl	Water		
0	1.000	0.0	0.000	0.000	8.328	0.000	32.0
2	1.004	0.6	0.528	0.044	8.318	0.044	31.5
4	1.007	1.1	1.056	0.089	8.297	0.089	31.1
6	1.011	1.6	1.584	0.133	8.287	0.134	30.5
8	1.015	2.1	2.112	0.178	8.275	0.179	30.0
10	1.019	2.7	2.640	0.224	8.262	0.226	29.3
12	1.023	3.3	3.167	0.270	8.250	0.273	28.8
14	1.026	3.7	3.695	0.316	8.229	0.320	28.2
16	1.030	4.2	4.223	0.362	8.216	0.367	27.6
18	1.034	4.8	4.751	0.409	8.202	0.415	27.0
20	1.038	5.3	5.279	0.456	8.188	0.464	26.4
22	1.042	5.8	5.807	0.503	8.175	0.512	25.7
24	1.046	6.4	6.335	0.552	8.159	0.563	25.1
26	1.050	6.9	6.863	0.600	8.144	0.614	24.4
28	1.054	7.4	7.391	0.649	8.129	0.665	23.7
30	1.058	7.9	7.919	0.698	8.113	0.716	23.0
32	1.062	8.5	8.446	0.747	8.097	0.768	22.3
34	1.066	9.0	8.974	0.797	8.081	0.821	21.6
36	1.070	9.5	9.502	0.847	8.064	0.875	20.9
38	1.074	10.0	10.030	0.897	8.047	0.928	20.2
40	1.078	10.5	10.558	0.948	8.030	0.983	19.4
42	1.082	11.0	11.086	0.999	8.012	1.039	18.7
44	1.086	11.5	11.614	1.050	7.994	1.094	17.9
46	1.090	12.0	12.142	1.102	7.976	1.151	17.1
48	1.094	12.5	12.670	1.154	7.957	1.208	16.2
50	1.098	12.9	13.198	1.207	7.937	1.266	15.4
60	1.118	15.3	15.837	1.475	7.836	1.568	10.9
70	1.139	17.7	18.477	1.753	7.733	1.888	5.7
80	1.160	20.0	21.116	2.040	7.620	2.229	-0.4
90	1.182	22.3	23.755	2.338	7.506	2.594	-1.1
100	1.204	24.6	26.395	2.647	7.380	2.987	30.0

1.5.8   Graph of Percentage Salt versus Degrees Twaddell for Brine Solutions

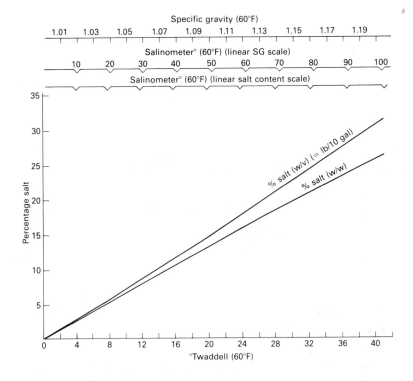

1.6   Irradiation Units

The ionising radiations which are of primary importance to the food processor are beta rays, x-rays and gamma rays. In particular gamma rays are electro-magnetic radiations continuously emitted from radionuclides such as caesium-137 and cobalt-60.

The SI unit of irradiation is the Gray (Gy) where

```
1 Gray (Gy)      =    100 rads
                 =    1 joule of energy absorbed per kg of absorber
1 Mrad           =    10 rads
1 Krad           =    10 rads
```

1.6.1   Radiation Preservation - Required Dosages of Radiation

Purpose	Dose Range (1000 rad)
Sterilisation	1000-5000
Pasteurisation	50-1000
Insect Disinfestation	5-100
Sprout-depressing	5-100

1.7   Vitamins - International Units

Report of the Sub-committee on Metrication of the British National Committee for Nutritional Sciences.

Section 14

Generic descriptions for the vitamins and equivalent quantities. In the following paragraphs, equivalent quantities of some compounds with vitamin activity have been suggested. The values given refer primarily to man and may not be applicable to other species.

```
1 µg retinol equivalent  = 1 µg retinol
                         = 1.147 ug retinyl acetate
                                 (International Standard)
                         = 6 µg B-carotene
                         = 12 µg other active carotenoids
                         = 3.33 iu vitamin A activity
```

(1 iu vitamin A activity = 0.3 µg retinol = 0.344 µg retinyl acetate [used for International Standard])

Section 16

Internationally agreed equivalent quantities for niacin. For niacin the summation is to be made in terms of nicotin-amide equivalents using the following factors:

$$1 \text{ mg nicotinamide equivalent} = 1 \text{ mg nicotinic amide}$$
$$= 1 \text{ mg nicotinic acid}$$
$$= 60 \text{ mg L- or DL-tryptophan}$$

Section 17

Tentative equivalent quantities for vitamin D. IUNS suggest for vitamin D summation in terms of chole-calciferol and the following factors are suggested for man:

$$1 \text{ ug cholecalciferol equivalent (man)} = 1 \text{ ug cholecalciferol}$$
$$= 1 \text{ ug ergocalciferol}$$
$$= 40 \text{ iu vitamin D activity}$$

Section 18

Tentative equivalent quantities for vitamin E. IUNS suggest for vitamin E summation in terms of tocopherol equivalents and the following factors are suggested:

$$1 \text{ mg a-tocopherol equivalent} = 1 \text{ mg D-a-tocopherol}$$
$$= 1.1 \text{ mg D-a-tocopherol acetate}$$
$$= 1.36 \text{ mg DL-a-tocopherol acetate}$$
$$= 1.49 \text{ iu vitamin E activity}$$

2 Engineering Data

2.1   Signs and Symbols Commonly Used in Food Engineering

Symbol	Property	Units
a	Acceleration	m/s^2
A	Aperture	mm
b	Breadth, width	−
c	Specific heat	J/kg K
D	Diameter	m
D	Diffusity	m^2/s
e	Basis of natural logarithms	−
E	Energy	J
f	Coefficient of friction	J/kg
F	Feed rate	kg/s
g	Acceleration due to gravity	m/s^2
G	Free energy	−
h	Coefficient of heat transfer	W/m^2 K
h	Enthalpy per unit weight	J/kg
H	Enthalpy	J/kg
H	Humidity	kg/kg
I	Moment of inertia	kg m
j	Heat transfer factor	−
J	Mechanical equivalent of heat	J/kg
K	Mass transfer factor	$kg/m^2 s$
L	Length	m
L	Liquid rate	kg/s
m	Mass	kg
m	Slope	−
M	Mesh	mm
N	Rate of rotation	rpm
N	Number of plates	−
P	Pressure	N/m^2
q	Volumetric flow rate	m^3/s
Q	Total heat transferred	W
r	Radius	m
R	Reduction ratio or reflux ratio	−
S	Entropy	J/kg
S	Solubility	kg/100 kg
T	Temperature	K
t	Time	s
u	Velocity	m/s
V	Volume	m^3
V_s	Humid volume	m^3/kg
W	Mass flow rate	kg/s
W	Water content	%
W	Residue, waste, bottoms, underflow	kg
x	Distance in direction of flow	m
X	Mole ration (liquid)	−
Y	Mole or mass fraction (vapour)	−
Z	Distance above datum	m

Greek Alphabet Symbol		Property	Units
α	alpha	Angle	degrees radians
α	alpha	Coefficient of linear expansion	m/m^2 K
α	alpha	Thermal diffusivity	m^2/s
α	alpha	Relative volatility	-
α	alpha	Specific cake resistance	-
β	beta	Coefficient of expansion (volumetric)	m/m^3 K
γ	gamma	Activity coefficient, radiation type	-
Δ	delta	Finite difference	-
ϵ	epsilon	Emissivity	-
η	eta	Efficiency	-
θ	theta	Temperature	K
κ	kappa	Ratio of specific heats	-
λ	lamda	Thermal conductivity	W/m K
μ	mu	Viscosity	kg/m s
ρ	rho	Density	kg/m^3
σ	sigma	Surface tension	-
τ	tau	Stress	N/m^2
φ	phi	Function	-
ω	omega	Solid angle	degrees radians
ω	omega	Angular velocity	rad/s
ω	omega	Linear expansion	m/m^2 K

Mathematical Signs and Symbols

$\pm$	plus or minus	dx	differential of x
$\sim$	proportional sign	d^2y/dx^2	second derivative of y with respect to x
$\nless$	not less than		
$\ngtr$	not greater than	$\int$	integral of
$\approx$	similar to	$/\ :$	divided by; ratio sign
$\neq$	not equal to	$\sqrt{}$	square root
∞	infinity	$\angle$	angle
$<$	less than	$f(x)$	function of x
$>$	greater than	$\sum$	summation of
$\cong$	approximately equal to		
$\equiv$	equivalent to	dy/dx	derivative of y with respect to x
$\propto$	varies as		
$\therefore$	therefore	$\partial y/\partial x$	partial derivative of y with respect to x
$n\sqrt{}$	n th root		
$\perp$	perpendicular to	$\int_a^b$	integral between the limits a and b
Δx	increment of x		

2.2 Properties of Gases

2.2.1 Properties of Gases at Atmospheric Pressure

Gas	Thermal conductivity W/m ^{0}C	Specific heat kJ/kg ^{0}C	Density kg/m^3	Temperature ^{0}C
Air	0.024	1.005	1.29	0
	0.031	1.005	0.94	100
Carbon dioxide	0.015	0.80	1.98	0
	0.022	0.92	1.46	100
Nitrogen	0.024	1.05	1.3	0
	0.031	–	–	100
Refrigerant 12	0.008	0.92	–	0
	0.014	–	–	100

2.2.2 Properties of Ideal Gases

Gas	Molecular Weight	R kJ/kg K	Cp kJ/kg K	Cv kJ/kg K
Air	28.97	0.287	1.0035	0.7665
Ar	39.94	0.208	0.5203	0.3122
CO_2	44.01	0.189	0.8418	0.6529
CO	28.01	0.297	0.0413	0.7445
He	4.00	2.077	5.1926	3.1156
H_2	2.02	4.124	14.2091	10.0849
CH_4	16.04	0.518	2.2537	1.7354
N_2	28.02	0.297	1.0416	0.7448
O_2	32.00	0.260	0.9216	0.6618
H_2O	18.02	0.461	1.8723	1.4108

2.2.3   Specific Heat of Gases

The appropriate specific heats of gases (Cp) at 1 atmosphere pressure. kJ/kg K

Temperature °C	Oxygen	Nitrogen	Air	Carbon Dioxide	Water Vapour
0	0.92	1.05	1.01	0.87	1.87
100	0.94	1.07	1.03	0.93	1.91
200	0.98	1.09	1.07	1.01	1.93
300	1.00	1.10	1.08	1.09	2.01
400	1.05	1.11	1.09	1.17	2.05
500	1.07	1.13	1.10	1.26	2.14

NB The specific heat of a gas at constant pressure Cp is greater than its specific heat at constant volume since work needs to be done in expanding the gas against the external pressure.

2.2.4   Physical Properties of Nitrogen

Molecular weight	28.02
Specific volume (20°C, 1 atm)	860 ml/g
Boiling point (1 atm)	-195.8 °C
Melting point (1 atm)	-209.9 °C
Density (gas, 20°C, 1 atm)	1.16 g/1
Density (liquid, bpt)	0.808 g/ml
Critical temperature	-147 °C
Critical pressure	34 bar(g)
Latent heat of vapourisation (at bpt)	1330 cal/g-mole
Solubility in water (20°C, 1 atm)	1.56 %vol
Specific gravity (air = 1)	0.963
Colourless	
Odourless	

2.3   Heats of Combustion

Organic compounds containing carbon and hydrogen, or together with oxygen, may be burnt in oxygen gas to yield carbon dioxide and (liquid) water as the sole products. The heat change accompanying the complete combustion of one mole of a compound, at a given temperature and 1 atmosphere pressure, is called the heat of combustion. The heats of combustion of solids and liquids are usually measured at constant volume in a 'bomb calorimeter'.

A number of methods have been proposed for the calculation of the heats of combustion, from a knowledge of the formula of the particular substance.   An examination of the heats of combustion of organic compounds reveals that isomeric substances have very similar values, and that in any homologous series there is a change of 150–160 kcal per mole per CH_2 group.

Compound	Formula	State	Heat of Combustion	
			H_2O/CO_2 (liq)(gas) KJ/kg	H_2O/CO_2 (gas)(gas) KJ/kg
Hydrogen	H_2	gas	141,880.6	120,033.8
Carbon	C	solid	32,782.2	–
Carbon monoxide	CO	gas	10,109.9	–
Methane	CH_4	gas	55,538.3	50,047.3
Ethane	C_2H_6	gas	51,913.0	47,518.5
Propane	C_3H_8	gas	50,381.9	46,386.4
Propane	C_3H_8	liquid	49,560.4	45,771.4
n–Butane	C_4H_{10}	gas	49,190.3	45,401.2
n–Hexane	C_6H_{14}	gas	48,711.3	45,133.7
n–Hexane	C_6H_{14}	liquid	47,980.1	44,766.1

2.4   The Calorific Values of Modern Fuels

Fuel	kJ/kg	Btu/lbm
Wood	20 470	8 800
Peat	20 930	9 000
Coal (lignite)	25 590	11 000
Coal (sub-bituminous)	29 070	12 500
Coal (bituminous)	34 890	15 000
Coal (anthracite)	30 240	14 000
Methane (natural gas)	50 010	21 500
Propane	46 350	19 930
Octane (gasolene)	44 800	19 260
Fuel oil (No 2)	45 520	19 570

NB   Natural gas is normally sold on a volume basis rather than on a mass basis, the heating value of methane is expressed as 33 750 kJ/m or 906 Btu/ft, (density 0.674 kg/m or 0.042 lbm/ft at 1 atm and 60 F).   Similarly, the heating value of gasolene is expressed as 34 870 kJ/litre or 125 000 Btu/gal.

The heating value of fuel oil (No 2) is 39 300 kJ/litre or 14 100 Btu/gal.

Temperature	Pressure	Enthalpy (sat vap)	Latent Heat	Specific Volume
°C	kPa	kJ/kg	kJ/kg	m³/kg
0	0.611	2501	2501	206
1	0.66	2503	2499	193
2	0.71	2505	2497	180
4	0.81	2509	2492	157
6	0.93	2512	2487	138
8	1.07	2516	2483	121
10	1.23	2520	2478	106
12	1.40	2523	2473	93.8
14	1.60	2527	2468	82.8
16	1.82	2531	2464	73.3
18	2.06	2534	2459	65.0
20	2.34	2538	2454	57.8
22	2.65	2542	2449	51.4
24	2.99	2545	2445	45.9
26	3.36	2549	2440	40.0
28	3.78	2553	2435	36.7
30	4.25	2556	2431	32.9
40	7.38	2574	2407	19.5
50	12.3	2592	2383	12.0
60	19.9	2610	2359	7.67
70	31.2	2627	2334	5.04
80	47.4	2644	2309	3.41
90	70.1	2660	2283	2.36
100	101.35	2676	2257	1.673
105	120.8	2684	2244	1.42
110	143.3	2692	2230	1.21
115	169.1	2699	2217	1.04
120	198.5	2706	2203	0.892
125	232.1	2714	2189	0.771
130	270.1	2721	2174	0.669
135	313.0	2727	2160	0.582
140	361.3	2734	2145	0.509
150	475.8	2747	2114	0.393
160	617.8	2758	2083	0.307
180	1002	2778	2015	0.194
200	1554	2793	1941	0.127

2.6   The Physical and Thermal Properties of "Thermex"

"Thermex" is the registered trade mark of a brand of heat transfer medium manufactured by the Petrochemicals Division of ICI Ltd.

"Thermex can be used either in the liquid or in the vapour phase, where it has the advantage of a lower vapour pressure than steam at the same temperature; its total operational range is from 20 °C to 400 °C.

"Thermex" as produced is a pale coloured liquid comprising the eutectic mixture of diphenyl oxide and diphenyl (in the ratio 73.5:26.5 % by weight).   It solidifies at 12 °C.

Physical Properties

Boiling point at 760 mm Hg	275 °C
Freezing point	12 °C
Flash point (Pensky-Martens)	116 °C (241 °F)
Fire point	128 °C
Auto ignition temperature	640 °C
Surface tension (20 °C)	43 dynes/cm
Specific resistivity (45 °C)	3.4×10^{11} ohm-cm

Specification

Crystallising point	11.5-12.5 °C
Distillation range (760 mm Hg)	
IBP (initial boiling point)	250 °C min
FBP (final boiling point)	260 °C max
Water % w/w	0.05 max
Total sulphur, ppm	25 max
Total chlorine, ppm	5 max

2.6.1 Thermodynamic Properties of "Thermex"

Temp °C	°F	Vapour kg/cm^3	Enthalpy kcal/kg		Heat of kcal/kg	Heat Capacity cal/g °C	Viscosity cp	Density g/ml	kg/m^3
20	068		3.0	94.1	91.1	.379	0.00	1.063	0.000
25	77		4.8	95.5	90.7	.382		1.059	
30	86		6.7	97.0	90.3	.385	3.30	1.055	
35	95		8.6	98.5	89.9	.389	2.92	1.050	
40	104		10.5	100.0	89.5	.392	2.60	1.046	.001
45	113		12.4	101.6	89.2	.395	2.34	1.042	.002
50	122		14.4	103.2	88.8	.399	2.12	1.038	.002
55	131		16.5	104.9	88.4	.402	1.94	1.033	.003
60	140		18.6	106.6	88.0	.406	1.77	1.029	.004
65	149		20.6	108.2	87.6	.409	1.62	1.025	.005
70	158		22.7	109.9	87.2	.413	1.48	1.021	.007
75	167		24.8	111.6	86.8	.416	1.37	1.016	.009
80	176		26.9	113.3	86.4	.419	1.27	1.012	.011
85	185		29.0	115.0	86.0	.423	1.18	1.008	.014
90	194		31.2	116.8	85.6	.426	1.11	1.003	.018
95	203		33.3	118.5	85.2	.429	1.04	.999	.023
100			35.4	120.2	84.8	.433	.97	.995	.028
105	121		37.6	122.0	84.4	.436	.92	.990	.036
110	230	.009	39.8	123.8	84.0	.439	.87	.986	.045
115	239	.011	42.0	125.7	83.7	.443	.82	.982	.057
120	248	.014	44.3	127.6	83.3	.446	.78	.977	.069
125	257	.018	46.5	129.4	82.9	.450	.74	.973	.086
130	266	.022	48.8	131.3	82.5	.453	.70	.969	.104
135	275	.027	51.1	133.2	82.1	.457	.67	.964	.127
140	284	.032	53.3	135.0	81.7	.460	.63	.960	.150
145	293	.039	55.7	137.	81.1	.0	.60	.955	.183
150	302	.047	58.0	138.8	80.8	.467	.57	.951	.216
160	320	.067	62.7	142.7	80.0	.473	.52	.942	.300
170	338	.095	67.5	146.8	79.3	.480	.48	.933	.410
180	356	.132	72.2	150.6	78.4	.487	.45	.924	.541
190	374	.180	77.1	154.7	77.6	.494	.42	.915	.709
200	392	.245	82.1	158.8	76.7	.501	.39	.905	.943
210	410	.325	87.2	163.0	75.8	.507	.36	.896	1.25
220	428	.423	92.3	167.2	74.9	.514	.34	.887	1.68
230	446	.547	97.6	171.6	74.0	.521	.31	.877	2.22
240	464	.699	102.8	175.8	73.0	.528	.29	.868	2.87
250	482	.882	108.2	180.2	72.0	.534	.27	.858	3.60

Data provided by ICI Marketing Division.

2.7   The Properties of Engineering Solids

2.7.1   The Properties of Metals and Non-Metals

Material	Thermal conductivity W/m ^{0}C	Specific heat kJ/kg ^{0}C	Density kg/m^3	Temperature ^{0}C
1. Metals				
Aluminium	220	0.87	2640	0
Brass	97	0.38	8650	0
Cast iron	55	0.42	7210	0
Copper	388	0.38	8900	0
Steel (mild)	45	0.47	7840	18
Steel (stainless)	21	0.48	7950	20
2. Non-metals				
Asbestos sheet	0.17	0.84	890	51
Brick	0.7	0.92	1760	20
Cardboard	0.07	1.26	640	20
Concrete	0.87	1.05	2000	20
Celluloid	0.21	1.55	1400	30
Cotton wool	0.04	1.26	80	30
Cork	0.043	1.55	160	30
Expanded rubber	0.04		72	0
Fibreboard	0.052		240	21
Glass, soda	0.52	0.84	2240	20
Ice	2.25	2.10	920	0
Mineral wool	0.04		145	30
Polyethylene	0.55	2.30	950	20
Polystyrene foam	0.036		24	0
Polyurethane foam	0.026		32	0
Polyvinyl chloride	0.29	1.30	1400	20
Wood shavings	0.09	2.50	150	0
Wood	0.28	2.50	700	30

2.7.2   The Properties of Miscellaneous Engineering Materials

Material	Thermal Conductivity W/m ^{0}C	Specific Heat kJ/kg ^{0}C	Density kg/m^3
Asbestos, cement board	0.61	0.84	1400
Asbestos, millboard	0.14	0.84	1000
Asphalt	–	1.67	1100
Beeswax	–	3.43	950
Brick, common	0.73	0.92	1750
Brick, hard	1.30	1.00	2000
Chalk	0.83	0.90	2000
Charcoal, wood	0.09	1.00	400
Coal, anthracite	–	1.26	1500
Coal, bituminous	–	1.38	1200
Concrete, light	0.43	0.96	1400
Concrete, stone	1.73	0.75	2200
Corkboard	0.04	1.88	200
Earth, dry	1.47	1.26	1400
Fiber hardboard	0.21	2.09	1100
Glass, window	0.95	0.84	2500
Gypsum board	0.17	1.09	800
Hairfelt	0.05	2.04	100
Leather, dry	0.16	1.51	900
Limestone	0.64	0.91	2500
Magnesia (85%)	0.07	0.84	250
Marble	2.60	0.88	2600
Mica	0.69	0.50	2700
Mineral wool blanket	0.043	0.84	100
Paper	0.12	1.38	900
Paraffin	0.26	2.89	900
Plaster, light	0.26	1.00	700
Plaster, sand	0.73	0.92	1800
Plastics, foamed	0.03	1.26	200
Plastics, solid	0.19	1.67	1200
Porcelain	1.6	0.92	2500
Sandstone	1.7	0.92	2300
Sawdust	0.09	0.88	150
Silica aerogel	0.026	0.84	110
Vermiculite	0.061	0.84	130
Wood, balsa	0.05	2.93	160
Wood, oak	0.17	2.09	700
Wood, white pine	0.12	2.51	500
Wood, felt	0.07	1.38	300
Wool, loose	0.03	1.26	100

Adapted from Handbook of Tables for Applied Engineering Science, CRC Press Inc.

2.7.3 Bulk Solid Materials Classification and Coding

The information and data contained in the following 'materials table' has been compiled by members of CEMA and represents many years of experience in the successful design and application of materials handling equipment. The table shows in the first column the range of density that can be experienced in handling that particular material. The next column contains the material code number, which consists of the average density, the usual size designation, the flowability number and the abrasive number followed by those material characteristics which are termed 'conveyability hazards'.

Thus a very fine 100 mesh material with an average bulk density of 50 lbs/ft^3 (801 kg/m^3), that has an average flowability and is moderately abrasive, would have a material code $50A_{100}36$. If this material was very dusty and mildly corrosive the material code number might then be $50A_{100}36LT$.

The 'materials table' includes data on various grains, seeds and agricultural feeds that are commonly handled in many conveyor types. The data given and in particular the materials factor Fm are for average conditions. For instance wheat when dry or with less than 10% moisture is very free-flowing, and the Fm factor of 0.4 is used. When higher moisture levels are prevalent a material factor of 0.5–0.6 is suggested.

The 'materials table' is used only as a guide, the indicated data has not been established as a result of precise laboratory tests but as a compilation of the experience of several conveyor manufacturers.

Key to Materials Table

Major class	Material characteristics		Code designation
Density	Bulk density, loose		Actual lbs/ft^3
Size	Very fine	No 200 sieve and under	A_{200}
		No 100 sieve and under	A_{100}
		No 40 sieve and under	A_{40}
	Fine	No 6 sieve and under	B_6
	Granular	$\frac{1}{2}$" and under	$C_{\frac{1}{2}}$
		3" and under	D_3
		7" and under	D_7
	Lumpy	16" and under	D_{16}
		Over 16" to be specified	
		X=Actual maximum size	D_x
	Irregular	Stringy, fibrous, cylindrical slabs, etc	E

Major class	Material characteristics	Code designation
Flowability	Very free flowing - flow function >10	1
	Free flowing - flow function >4 but <10	2
	Average flowability - flow function >2 but <4	3
	Sluggish - flow function <2	4
Abrasiveness	Mildly abrasive - index 1-17	5
	Moderately abrasive - index 18-67	6
	Extremely abrasive - index 68-416	7
Miscellaneous Properties or Hazards	Builds up and hardens	F
	Generates static electricity	G
	Decomposes - deteriorates in storage	H
	Flammability	J
	Becomes plastic or tends to soften	K
	Very dusty	L
	Aerates and becomes fluid	M
	Explosiveness	N
	Stickiness-adhesion	O
	Contaminable, affecting use	P
	Degradable, affecting use	Q
	Gives off harmful or toxic gas or fumes	R
	Highly corrosive	S
	Mildly corrosive	T
	Hygroscopic	U
	Interlocks, mats or agglomerates	V
	Oils present	W
	Packs under pressure	X
	Very light and fluffy - may be windswept	Y
	Elevated temperature	Z

NB   Those materials showing x may be handled in vertical screw conveyors.   To convert lbs/ft^3 to kg/m^3 multiply by 16.018.

Material	Weight lbs/ft^3	Material Code	Series	Material Factor Fm	V
Adipic acid	45	$45A_{100}35$	2B	0.5	x
Alfalfa meal	14-22	$18B_6 45WY$	2D	0.6	x
Alfalfa pellets	41-43	$42C_{\frac{1}{2}}25$	2D	0.5	
Alfalfa seed	10-15	$13B_6 15N$	1A-1B-1C	0.4	x
Almonds, broken	27-30	$29C_{\frac{1}{4}}35Q$	2D	0.9	
Almonds, whole, shelled	28-30	$29C_{\frac{1}{4}}35Q$	2D	0.9	
Alum, fine	45-50	$48B_6 35U$	1A-1B-1C	0.6	
Alum, lump	50-60	$55B_6 25$	2A-2B	1.4	
Alumina	55-65	$58B_6 27MY$	3D	1.8	
Alumina fines	35	$35A_{100}27MY$	3D	1.6	
Aluminium oxide	60-120	$90A_{100}17M$	3D	1.8	
Baking powder	40-55	$48A_{100}35$	1B	0.6	x
Baking soda	40-55	$48A_{100}25$	1B	0.6	x
Barley, fine, ground	24-38	$31B_6 35$	1A-1B-1C	0.4	x
Barley, malted	31	$31C_{\frac{1}{2}}35$	1A-1B-1C	0.4	x
Barley, meal	28	$28C_{\frac{1}{2}}$	1A-1B-1C	0.4	x
Barley, whole	36-48	$42B_6 25N$	1A-1B-1C	0.5	x
Blood dried	35-45	$40D_3 45U$	2D	2.0	x
Blood, ground, dried	30	$30A_{100}35U$	1A-1B	1.0	x
Bran, rice-rye-wheat	16-20	$18B_6 35NY$	1A-1B-1C	0.5	
Bread crumbs	20-25	$23B_6 35PQ$	1A-1B-1C	0.6	
Brewers grain,spent,dry	14-30	$22C_{\frac{1}{4}}45$	1A-1B-1C	0.5	x
Brewers grain,spent,wet	55-60	$58C_{\frac{1}{4}}45T$	2A-2B	0.8	
Buckwheat	37-42	$40B_6 25N$	1A-1B-1C	0.4	x
Calcium lactate	26-29	$28D_3 45QTR$	2A-2B	0.6	
Casein	36	$36B_6 35$	2D	1.6	
Cashew nuts	32-37	$35C_{\frac{1}{4}}45$	2D	0.7	
Chocolate, cake,pressed	40-45	$43D_3 25$	2B	1.5	
Cocoa beans	30-45	$38C_{\frac{1}{4}}25Q$	1A-1B	0.5	
Cocoa nibs	35	$35C_{\frac{1}{4}}25$	2D	0.5	
Cocoa, powdered	30-35	$33A_{100}45XY$	1B	0.9	
Cocoanut, shredded	20-22	$21E45$	2B	1.5	x
Coffee, chaff	20	$20B_6 25MY$	1A-1B	1.0	x
Coffee, green bean	25-32	$29C_{\frac{1}{4}}25PQ$	1A-1B	0.5	
Coffee, ground, dry	25	$25A_{40}35P$	1A-1B	0.6	x
Coffee, ground, wet	35-45	$40A_{40}45X$	1A-1B	0.6	
Coffee, roasted	20-30	$25C_{\frac{1}{4}}25PQ$	1B	0.4	x
Coffee, soluble	19	$19A_{40}35PUY$	1B	0.4	x
Copra, cake, ground	40-45	$43B_6 45HW$	1A/B/C	0.7	x
Copra, cake, lumpy	25-30	$28D_3 35HW$	2A/B/C	0.8	
Copra, meal	40-45	$42B_6 35HW$	2D	0.7	x
Corn, cracked	40-50	$45B_6 25P$	1A/B/C	0.6	
Corn cobs, ground	17	$17C_{\frac{1}{4}}25Y$	1A/B/C	0.6	
Corn cobs, whole	12-15	$14E35$	2A-2B		
Corn ear	56	$56E35$	2A-2B		
Corn germ	21	$21B_6 35PY$	1A/B/C	0.4	x
Corn grits	40-45	$43B_6 35P$	1A/B/C	0.5	x
Corn meal	32-40	$36B_6 35P$	1A-1B	0.5	x
Corn oil cake	25	$25D_7 45HW$	1A-1B	0.6	x

Material	Weight lbs/ft^3	Material Code	Series	Material Factor Fm	V
Corn seed	45	$45C_125PQ$	1A–1B–1C	0.4	
Corn shelled	45	$45C_125$	1A–1B–1C	0.4	x
Corn sugar	30–45	$33B_635PU$	1B	1.0	x
Cottonseed, cake	40–45	$43C_145HW$	1A–1B	1.0	x
Cottonseed, meal	25–30	$28B_645HW$	3A–3B	0.5	x
Egg powder	16	$16A_{40}35MPY$	1B	1.0	
Fish meal	35–40	$38C_145HP$	1A–1B–1C	1.0	x
Fish scrap	40–50	$45D_745H$	1A–1B–1C	1.5	
Flour wheat	33–40	$37A_{40}45L\ P$	1B	0.6	
Fullers earth, dry	30–40	$35A_{40}25$	2D	2.0	
Fullers earth, spent, dry	60–65	$63C_1450W$	3D	2.0	
Gelatine, granular	32	$32B_235PU$	1B	0.8	
Gluten, meal	40	$40B_635P$	1B	0.6	
Hay, chopped	8–12	$10C_135JY$	2A–2B	1.6	
Hops, spent, dry	35	$35D_335$	2A–2B–2C	1.0	x
Hops, spent, wet	50–55	$53D_345V$	2A–2B	1.5	
Ice, crushed	35–45	$40D_3350$	2A–2B	0.4	
Ice, flaked	40–45	$43C_1350$	1B	0.6	x
Ice, cubes	33–35	$34D_3350$	1B	0.4	x
Lactose	32	$32A_{40}35PU$	1B	0.6	
Malt, dry, ground	20–30	$25B_635NP$	1A–1B–1C	0.5	x
Malt, meal	36–40	$38B_625P$	1A–1B–1C	0.4	x
Malt, dry, whole	20–30	$25C_135N$	1A–1B–1C	0.5	x
Malt, sprouts	13–15	$14C_135P$	1A–1B–1C	0.4	x
Meat, ground	50–55	$53E45HQTX$	2A–2B	1.5	
Meat, scrap	40	$40E46H$	2D	1.5	
Milk, dried, flake	5–6	$6B_635PUY$	1B	0.4	
Milk, malted	27–30	$29A_{40}45PX$	1B	0.9	
Milk, powdered	20–45	$33B_625PM$	1B	0.5	
Milk sugar	32	$32A_{100}35PX$	1B	0.6	
Milk, whole, powder	20–36	$28B_635PUX$	1B	0.5	
Mill scale (steel)	120–125	$123E46T$	3D	3.0	
Mustard seed	45	$45B_615N$	1A–1B–1C	0.4	x
Niacin	35	$35A_{40}35P$	2D	0.8	
Oats	26	$26C_125MN$	1A–1B–1C	0.4	x
Oats, crushed	22	$22B_645NY$	1A–1B–1C	0.6	x
Oats, flour	35	$35A_{100}35$	1A–1B–1C	0.5	x
Oats, hulls	8–12	$10B_635NY$	1A–1B–1C	0.5	x
Oats, rolled	19–24	$22C_135NY$	1A–1B–1C	0.6	x
Oleo margarine	59	$59E45HKPWX$	2A–2B	0.4	
Orange peel, dry	15	$15E45$	2A–2B	1.5	
Peanuts (in shell)	15–20	$18D_335Q$	2A–2B	0.6	
Peanut meal	30	$30B_635P$	1B	0.6	x
Peanuts, raw	15–20	$18D_336Q$	3D	0.7	
Peanuts, shelled	35–45	$40C_135Q$	1B	0.4	x
Peas, dried	45–50	$48C_115NQ$	1A–1B–1C	0.5	x
Polystyrene beads	40	$40B_635PQ$	1B	0.4	
PVC powder	20–30	$25A_{100}45KT$	2B	1.0	
PVC pellets	20–30	$25E45KPQT$	1B	0.6	

continued over

Material	Weight lbs/ft^3	Material Code	Series	Material Factor F_m	V
Polyethylene pellets	30–35	$33C_{\frac{1}{2}}45Q$	1A–1B	0.4	x
Potato flour	48	$48A_{200}35MNP$	1A–1B	0.5	x
Rice, bran	20	$20B_{6}35NY$	1A–1B–1C	0.4	x
Rice, grits	42–45	$44B_{6}35P$	1A–1B–1C	0.4	x
Rice, polished	30	$30C_{\frac{1}{2}}15P$	1A–1B–1C	0.4	x
Rice, hulled	45–49	$47C_{\frac{1}{2}}25P$	1A–1B–1C	0.4	x
Rice hulls	20–21	$21B_{6}35NY$	1A–1B–1C	0.4	x
Rice, rough	32–36	$34C_{\frac{1}{2}}35N$	1A–1B–1C	0.6	x
Rye	42–48	$45B_{6}15N$	1A–1B–1C	0.4	x
Rye bran	15–20	$18B_{6}35Y$	1A–1B–1C	0.5	x
Rye meal	35–40	$38B_{6}35$	1A–1B–1C	0.5	x
Safflower meal	50	$50B_{6}35$	1A–1B–1C	0.6	x
Safflower seed	45	$45B_{6}15N$	1A–1B–1C	0.4	x
Salt, dry, coarse	45–60	$53C_{\frac{1}{2}}36TU$	3D	1.0	x
Salt, dry, fine	70–80	$75B_{6}36TU$	3D	1.7	x
Sesame seed	27–41	$34B_{6}26$	2D	0.6	x
Soda ash, heavy	55–65	$60B_{6}36$	2D	1.0	
Soda ash, light	20–35	$28A_{40}36Y$	2D	0.8	x
Sodium nitrate	70–80	$75D_{3}25NS$	2A–2B	1.2	
Soybean cake	40–43	$42D_{3}35W$	2A–1B–1C	1.0	x
Soybean flour	27–30	$29A_{40}35MN$	1A–1B–1C	0.8	x
Soybean meal (hot)	40	$40B_{6}35T$	2A–2B	0.5	
Starch	25–50	$38A_{40}15M$	1A–1B–1C	1.0	x
Sugar beet, pulp, dry	12–15	$14C_{\frac{1}{2}}26$	2D	0.9	
Sugar beet, pulp, wet	25–45	$35C_{\frac{1}{2}}35X$	1A–1B–1C	1.2	
Sugar, refined, granulated, dry	50–55	$53B_{6}35PU$	1B	1.0–1.2	x
Sugar, refined, granulated, wet	55–65	$60C_{\frac{1}{2}}35X$	1B	1.4–2.0	
Sugar, powdered	50–60	$55A_{100}35PX$	1B	0.8	x
Sugar, raw	55–65	$60B_{6}35PX$	1B	1.5	
Sunflower seed	19–38	$29C_{\frac{1}{2}}15$	1A–1B–1C	0.5	x
Tricalcium phosphate	40–50	$45A_{40}45$	1A–1B	1.6	
Trisodium phosphate, granule	60	$60B_{6}36$	2D	1.7	
TSP pulverised	50	$50A_{40}36$	2D	1.6	x
Walnut shells	35–45	$40B_{6}36$	2D	1.0	x
Wheat	45–48	$47_{\frac{1}{2}}25N$	1A–1B–1C	0.4	x
Wheat, cracked	40–45	$43B_{6}25N$	1A–1B–1C	0.4	x
Wheat, germ	18–28	$23B_{6}25$	1A–1B–1C	0.4	x

2.7.4 Fluidisation Data – Air Velocities Required for Fluid Conveying

Bulk Density kg/m³	Air Velocity m/s	Bulk Density kg/m³	Air Velocity m/s
160	14.7	1120	39.1
240	18.2	1200	40.6
320	20.9	1280	41.9
400	23.4	1360	43.2
480	25.7	1440	44.2
560	27.9	1520	45.7
640	29.7	1600	46.7
720	31.4	1680	48.0
800	33.0	1760	49.3
880	34.5	1840	52.0
960	36.3	1920	53.3
1040	37.8		

2.8 Standard Sieve Data

Details are given below of the most widely used mesh sizes.   The British and US standard sizes differ only slightly.

Mesh No	Size of Opening (in)	Open Area (%)	Wire Diam (in)	Equiv Nylon Cloth No	Aperture Size (μ)
20	0.0340	46.2	0.016	860	860
30	0.0198	35.3	0.0135	505	505
40	0.0150	36.0	0.010	390	390
60	0.0087	27.2	0.008	223	223
80	0.0070	31.4	0.0055	183	183
100	0.0055	30.3	0.0045	130	130
120	0.0046	30.7	0.0037	116	116
150	0.0041	37.4	0.0026	102	102
180	0.0033	34.7	0.0023	86	86
200	0.0029	33.6	0.0021	73	73
250	0.0024	36.0	0.0016	64	64
325	0.0017	30.0	0.0014	44	44

2.9 Standard Pipe Dimensions and Data

Tube diameters in the range 16mm to 50mm are used. The mechanical design features and other data is covered by the British Standard, BS 3274. The standards of the American Tubular Heat Exchanger Manufacturers Association, the TEMA standards, are also universally used.

Standard Dimensions for Steel Tubes

Outside Diameter mm	Wall Thickness mm				
16	1.2	1.6	2.0	–	–
20	–	1.6	2.0	2.6	–
25	–	1.6	2.0	2.6	3.2
30	–	1.6	2.0	2.6	3.2
38	–	–	2.0	2.6	3.2
50	–	–	2.0	2.6	3.2

2.10   Materials of Construction.   Food Grade Materials

Composition of Some Types of Stainless Steel

Composition	Type					
	302	304	316	430	440C	502
Carbon	0.08-0.20	0.08	0.10	0.12	0.95	0.10
Manganese	2.00	2.00	2.00	1.00	1.00	1.00
Phosporus	0.04	0.04	0.04	0.04	0.04	0.04
Sulphur	0.03	0.03	0.03	0.03	0.03	0.03
Silicon	1.00	1.00	1.00	1.00	1.00	1.00
Nickel	8.00-10.00	8-10	10-14	0.00	0.00	0.00
Chromium	17.00-19.00	18-20	16-18	14-18	16-18	4.0-6.0
Molybdenum	0.00	0.00	2.00-3.00	0.00	0.75	0.00

Commonly Used Grades of Austenitic Stainless Steel

BS 1501	AISI	C max	Si max	Mn max	Cr range	Ni range	Mo	Ti
801B	304	0.08	-	2.00	17.5-20	8.0-11	-	-
810C	304 ELC	0.03	1.00	2.00	17.5-20	10 min	-	-
801 Ti	321	0.12	1.00	2.00	17-20	7.5min	-	4xC
801 Nb	347	0.08	1.00	2.00	17-20	9 min	-	-
821 Ti	-	0.12	1.00	2.00	17-20	25min	-	4xC
845 B	316	0.08	1.00	2.00	16.5-18.5	10min	2.25-3	4xC
845 Ti	-	0.08	0.06	2.00	16.5-18.5	10min	2.25-3	4xC
846	-	0.08	1.00	2.00	18-20	11-14	3-4	-

NB   801 Nb - 10 x C level of Nb.   S & P 0.0045 % all grades.
AISI   American Iron & Steel Institute.

Source: Chemical Engineering, Coulsen & Richardson, Vol 6.

The Mechanical Properties of the Austenitic Stainless Steels

The austenitic stainless steels have greater strength than the plain carbon steels, particularly at elevated temperatures.   Austenitic stainless steels do not become brittle at low temperatures unlike the plain carbon steels and in the annealed condition they are non-magnetic.

Typical Design stress N/mm2	300°C	400°C	500°C	600°C
Mild steel	77	62	31	-
Stainless 18/8	108	100	92	62

General Corrosion Resistance of Stainless Steels

The higher the alloying content, the better the corrosion resistance over a wide range of conditions, (strongly oxidising to reducing), but the higher the cost. A ranking order in terms of corrosion resistance, taking type 304 as unity, is given below;

304	304L	321	316	316L	310
1.0	1.1	1.1	1.25	1.3	1.6

Intergrannular corrosion, (weld decay) and stress corrosion cracking are problems associated with the use of stainless steels.   In general, stainless steels are used for corrosion resistance when oxidising conditions exist.

Source: Chemical Engineering, Vol 6, Design, J M Coulson, J F Richardson and R K Sinnot. Pergamon Press, Oxford, England.

2.11 The Physical Properties of Refrigerants

The physical properties of the refrigerant fluids used in the food industry are presented in the following section. The data is arranged in the format shown below:

2.11.1 Classification of Refrigerants

Refrig-erant No	Chemical Name	Formula	Molec-ular Weight	Boiling Point °C
Halocarbon Compounds				
10	Carbontetrachloride	CCl_4	153.8	170.2
11	Trichloromonofluoro-methane	CCl_3F	137.4	74.8
12	Dichlorodifluoromethane	CCl_2F_2	120.9	-21.6
13	Monochlorotrifluoro-methane	$CClF_3$	104.5	-114.6
13B1	Monobromotrifluoromethane	$CBrF_3$	148.9	-72.0
14	Carbontetrafluoride	CF_4	88.0	-198.4
20	Chloroform	$CHCl_3$	119.4	142
21	Dichloromonofluoromethane	$CHCl_2F$	102.9	48.1
22	Monochlorodifluoromethane	$CHClF_2$	86.5	-41.4
23	Trifluoromethane	CHF_3	70.0	-119.9
30	Methylene chloride	CH_2Cl_2	84.9	105.2
31	Monochloromonofluoro-methane	CH_2ClF	68.5	48.0
32	Methylene fluoride	CH_2F_2	52.0	-61.4
40	Methyl Chloride	CH_3Cl	50.5	-10.8
41	Methyl fluoride	CH_3F	34.0	-109
50	Methane†	CH_4	16.0	-259
110	Hexachloroethane	CCl_3CCl_3	236.8	365
111	Pentachloromonofluoro-methane	CCl_3CCl_2F	220.3	279
112	Tetrachlorodifluoroethane	CCl_2FCCl_2F	203.8	199.0
112a	Tetrachlorodifluoroethane	CCl_3CClF_2	203.8	195.8
113	Trichlorotrifluoroethane	CCl_2FCClF_2	187.4	117.6
113a	Trichlorotrifluoroethane	CCl_3CF_3	187.4	114.2
114	Dichlorotetrafluoroethane	$CClF_2CClF_2$	170.9	38.4
114a	Dichlorotetrafluoroethane	CCl_2FCF_3	170.9	38.5
114B2	Dibromotetrafluoroethane	$CBrF_2CBrF_2$	259.9	117.5
115	Monochloropentafluoro-ethane	$CClF_2CF_3$	154.5	-37.7
116	Hexafluoroethane	CF_3CF_3	138	-108.8
120	Pentachloroethane	$CHCl_2CCl_3$	202.3	324
123	Dichlorotrifluoroethane	$CHCl_2CF_3$	153	83.7
124	Monochlorotetrafluoro-ethane	$CHClFCF_3$	136.5	10.4

continued over

Refrigerant No	Chemical Name	Formula	Molecular Weight	Boiling Point °C
124a	Monochlorotetrafluoroethane	CHF_2CClF_2	136.5	14
125	Pentafluoroethane	CHF_2CF_3	120	-55
133a	Monochlorotrifluoroethane	CH_2ClCF_3	118.5	43
140a	Trichloroethane	CH_3CCl_3	133.4	165
142b	Monochlorodifluoroethane	CH_3CClF_2	100.5	12.2
143a	Trifluoroethane	CH_3CF_3	84	-53.5
150a	Dichloroethane	CH_3CHCl_2	98.9	140
152a	Difluoroethane	CH_3CHF_2	66	-12.4
160	Ethyl chloride	CH_3CH_2Cl	64.5	54
170	Ethane †	CH_3CH_3	30	-127.5
218	Octofluoropropane	$CF_3CF_2CF_3$	188	-36.4
290	Propane	$CH_2CH_2CH_3$	44	-44.2

Cyclic Organic Compounds

C316	Dichlorohexafluorocyclobutane	$C_4Cl_2F_6$	233	140
C317	Monochloroheptafluorocyclobutane	C_4ClF_7	216.5	77
C318	Octafluorocyclobutane	C_4F_8	200	21.1

Azeotropes

500	Refrig 12/152a	CCl_2F_2/CH_3CHF_2	99.29	-28
501	Refrig 22/12	$CHClF_2/CCl_2F_2$	93.1	-42
502	Refrig 22/15	$CHClF_2/CClF_2CF_3$	112	-50.1
503	Refrig 23/13	$CHF_3/CClF_3$	87.5	-126.1
504	Refrig 32/115	CH_2F_2/CCl_2CF_3	79.9	-71

Miscellaneous Organic Compounds Hydrocarbons

600	Butane	$CH_3CH_2CH_2CH_3$	58.1	31.3
601	Isobutane	$CH(CH_3)_3$	58.1	14
1150	Ethylene †	$CH_2=CH_2$	28	-155
1270	Propylene †	$CH_3CH=CH_2$	42.1	-53.7

Oxygen Compounds

610	Ethyl ether	$C_2H_5OC_2H_5$	74.1	94.3
611	Methyl formate	$HCOOCH_3$	60	89.2

† The compounds methane and ethane appear under the halocarbon section although they are hydrocarbons and therefore should be in the same section as ethylene and propylene.

Refrigerant No	Chemical Name	Formula	Molecular Weight	Boiling Point ^{0}C
Nitrogen Compounds				
630	Methyl amine	CH_3NH_2	31.1	20.3
631	Ethyl amine	$C_2H_5NH_2$	45.1	61.8
Inorganic Compounds				
717	Ammonia	NH_3	17	-28
718	Water	H_2O	18	212
729	Air		29	-318
744	Carbon dioxide	CO_2	44	-109
744A	Nitrous oxide	N_2O	44	-127
764	Sulphur dioxide	SO_2	64	14
Unsaturated Organic Compounds				
1112a	Dichlorodifluoro-ethylene	$CCl=CF_2$	133	67
1113	Monochlorotrifluoro-ethylene	$CClF=CF_2$	116.5	-18.2
1114	Tetrafluoroethylene	$CF_2=CF_2$	100	-105
1120	Trichloroethylene	$CHCl=CCl_2$	131.4	187
1130	Dichloroethylene	$CHCl=CHCl$	96.9	118
1132a	Vinylidene fluoride	$CH_2=CF_2$	64	-119
1140	Vinyl chloride	$CH_2=CHCl$	62.5	7
1141	Vinyl fluoride	$CH_2=CHF$	46	-98

2.11.2   Properties of Sodium Chloride Brine

Sp Gr at 4°C (39°F)	Degrees Baumè at 15.6°C (60°F)	Degrees Salometer at 15.6°C (60°F)	Pounds of salt per ft³	% salt Weight	Freezing Point °C	Freezing Point °F	Specific Heat kJ/kg°C
1.007	1	4	0.628	1	0	31.8	4.153
1.015	2	8	1.264	2	-1.7	29.3	4.119
1.023	3	12	1.914	3	-2	27.8	4.086
1.030	4	16	2.573	4	-3	26.6	4.052
1.037	5	20	3.238	5	-4	25.2	4.019
1.045	6	24	3.912	6	-4	23.9	3.960
1.053	7	28	4.615	7	-5	22.5	3.901
1.061	8	32	5.295	8	-6	21.2	3.847
1.068	9	36	5.998	9	-7	19.9	3.788
1.076	10	40	6.709	10	-7	18.7	3.734
1.091	12	48	8.618	12	-9	16.0	3.659
1.115	15	60	10.389	15	-11	12.2	3.579
1.155	20	80	14.421	20	-14	6.1	3.470
1.187	24	96	17.772	24	-17	1.2	3.328
1.196	25	100	18.610	25	-18	0.5	3.278
1.204	26	104	19.522	26	-17	1.1	3.227

NB   To convert from 'Pounds of Salt per Ft³' to Pounds of salt per gallon of solution, since 1 US gallon $\equiv 1.337 \times 10^{-1} ft^3$, and 1 UK gallon $\equiv 1.6054 \times 10^{-1} ft^3$;

then 0.628 'Pounds of Salt per ft³' $\equiv$ $0.628 \times 1.337 \times 10^{-1}$ Pounds salt/US gallon

$\equiv$ 0.084 Pounds salt/US gallon

$\equiv$ 0.101 Pounds salt/UK gallon

2.11.3   Properties of Calcium Chloride Brine

Degrees Baumé 15.6°C (60°F)	Degrees Salometer 15.6°C (60°F)	Specific Gravity 15.6°C (60°F)	% CaCl$_2$ by weight	Freezing Point °C	°F	Specific Heat kJ/kg °C
0	0	1.000	0	0	32	4.1868
1	4	1.007	1	-0.6	31.1	4.145
2.1	8	1.015	2	-1	30.4	4.061
3.4	12	1.024	3	-1	29.5	4.019
4.5	16	1.032	4	-2	28.6	3.936
5.7	22	1.041	5	-2	27.7	3.894
6.8	26	1.049	6	-3	26.6	3.810
8	32	1.058	7	-4	25.5	3.768
9.1	36	1.067	8	-4	24.3	3.684
10.2	40	1.076	9	-5	22.8	3.643
11.4	44	1.085	10	-6	21.3	3.601
12.5	48	1.094	11	-7	19.7	3.517
13.5	52	1.103	12	-8	18.1	3.475
14.6	58	1.112	13	-9	16.3	3.433
15.6	62	1.121	14	-10	14.3	3.412
16.8	68	1.131	15	-11	12.2	3.329
17.8	72	1.140	16	-12	10	3.266
19	76	1.151	17	-13	7.5	3.224
20	80	1.160	18	-15	4.6	3.161
21	84	1.160	19	-17	1.7	3.098
22	88	1.179	20	-18	1.4	3.056
23	92	1.188	21	-21	-4.9	3.014
24	96	1.198	22	-23	-8.6	2.973
25	100	1.208	23	-24	-11.6	2.931
26	104	1.218	24	-27	-17.1	2.889
27	108	1.229	25	-30	-21.8	2.868
28	112	1.239	26	-33	-27	2.847
29	116	1.250	27	-36	-32.6	2.805
30	120	1.261	28	-39	-39.2	2.784
31	124	1.272	29	-43	-46.2	2.763
32	128	1.283	30	-48	-54.4	2.721

2.11.4 Theoretical Performance of Halocarbon Refrigerants – 40 °F Evaporating 100 °F Condensing

Property	R11	R-12	R-13B1	R-21
Superheat temperature °F	65	65	65	65
Evaporator pressure psig	15.6	37.0	123.9	4.8
Condenser pressure psig	8.8	117.2	300.6	25.3
Compression ratio	3.34	2.55	2.27	3.25
Net refrigerating effect Btu/lb	71.48	54.27	30.56	93.44
Refrigerant circulated lbs/min	2.798	3.685	6.545	21.40
Specific volume of vapour ft^3/lb	5.724	0.828	0.232	4.749
Compressor displacement ft^3/min	16.014	3.050	1.516	10.164
Horsepower	0.63	0.66	0.76	0.69
COP	7.530	7.100	6.203	6.901
Discharge temperature °F	139.2	133.0	137.5	167.0

NB To convert Btu/lb to J/kg multiply by 2.326 x 10^3.

2.12   Heat Transfer Data

2.12.1   Predicted Heat Transfer Coefficients

Process Condition	Heat Transfer Coefficient W/m^2 K
Still air or naturally circulating	
Air, freezing	5-10
Air, blast freezing	17-30
Plate contact freezer	50-150
Liquid immersion freezing	550
Brine, circulating	55-85
Liquid nitrogen freezing	150-500
Superheated steam or air	25-300
Oil, forced convection	55-1500
Water, forced convection	280-1200
Water, boiling	$1.7-57 \times 10^3$
Steam, dropwise condensing	$28.4-114 \times 10^3$
Steam, film-type condensing	$5.7-17 \times 10^3$
Organic vapour, condensing	$1.1-2.3 \times 10^3$
Surface cooler, (milk to water)	990
Gravity pasteurizer	850
Jacketed kettle, stirred	1.7×10^3
Jacketed kettle, evaporating	2.8×10^3
Vacuum pan, evaporating	2.8×10^3
Flash pasteurizer	3.4×10^3

2.12.2 Typical Values for Fouling Factors

Fluid	Coefficient W/m² °C
River water	3000-12000
Sea water	1000-3000
Cooling water (towers)	3000-6000
Towns water (soft)	3000-5000
Towns water (hard)	1000-2000
Steam condensate	1500-5000
Steam (oil free)	4000-10000
Steam (oil traces)	2000-5000
Refrigerated brine	3000-5000
Air and industrial gases	5000-10000
Flue gases	2000-5000
Organic vapours	5000
Organic liquids	5000
Light hydrocarbons	5000
Heavy hydrocarbons	2000
Boiling organics	2500
Condensing organics	5000
Heat transfer fluids	5000
Aqueous salt solutions	3000-5000

NB These values which are for shell and tube heat exchangers with plain (not finned) tubes, are taken from 'Chemical Engineering', Vol 6, by J M Coulson and J F Richardson.

2.12.3 Properties of Some Heat Exchange Liquids

Heat Exchange Liquid	Bpt °C	Specific Heat J/kg °C	Thermal Conductivity W/m °C	Enthalpy above 0 °C	Range °C
Water	100	4.2×10^3	0.684	627.0	0-204
o-Dichloro Benzene	-	2.3	0.111	500.7	0-260
Mineral Oil	-	2.3	0.116	314.0	10-299
Organo Silicate	>316	2.01	0.125	167.5	10-316
Chlorinated Diphenyl	>316	1.30	0.093	180.5	10-316
Diphenyl/ Diphenyl Oxide	260	2.20	0.132	578.4	20-370

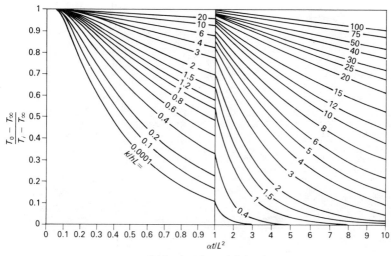

Heisler chart for an infinite plate.

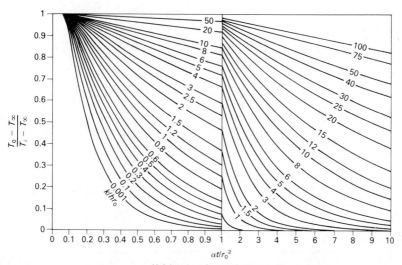

Heisler chart for a infinite cylinder.

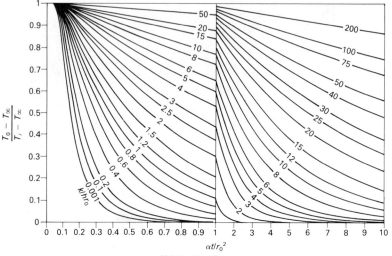

Heisler chart for a sphere.

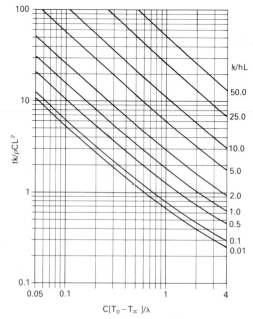

Freezing and thawing plot for an infinite plate.

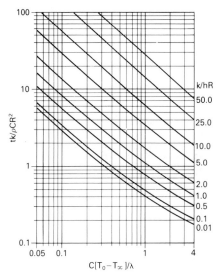

Freezing and thawing plot for an infinite cylinder

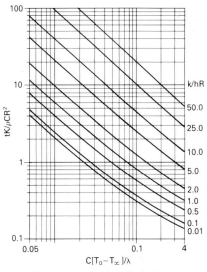

Freezing and thawing plot for a sphere.

2.14   Thermocouple Voltage Data

Temperature		Chrome-Alumel	Iron-Constantan	Copper-Constantan
°C	°F	(Mv)	(Mv)	(Mv)
-129	-200	-4.29	-5.76	-4.111
-101	-150	-3.52	-4.68	-3.380
-73.3	-100	-2.65	-3.49	-2.559
-45.6	-50	-1.70	-2.22	-1.654
-40	-40	-1.50	-1.96	-1.463
-28.9	-20	-1.10	-1.43	-1.072
	0	-0.68	-0.89	-0.670
-6.67	20	-0.20	-0.34	-0.254
4.44	40	0.18	0.22	0.171
15.6	60	0.62	0.79	0.609
26.7	80	1.06	1.36	1.057
37.8	100	1.52	1.94	1.517
49	120	1.97	2.52	1.987
60	140	2.43	3.11	2.467
71	160	2.89	3.71	2.958
82	180	3.36	4.31	3.458
93	200	3.82	4.91	3.967
104	220	4.28	5.51	4.486
116	240	4.74	6.11	5.014
127	260	5.20	6.72	5.550
138	280	5.65	7.33	6.094
149	300	6.09	7.94	6.647
177	350	7.20	9.48	8.064
204	400	8.31	11.03	9.525
232	450	9.43	12.57	11.030
260	500	10.57	14.12	12.575
316	600	12.86	17.18	15.773
371	700	15.18	20.26	19.100

Operation or Area	Footcandles (Minimum on the task at all times)
Bakeries	
Mixing room	50
Fermentation room	30
Make-up room (bread)	30
Sweet yeast raised products	50
Proofing room	30
Oven room	30
Fillings and other ingredients	30
Decorating and icing	
Hand	100
Mechanical	50
Wrapping room	30
Breweries	
Brew house	30
Boiling and keg washing	30
Filling (bottles, cans, kegs)	50
Confectionery and candy manufacture	
Box department	50
Chocolate department	
Husking, winnowing, fat extraction, crushing and refining, feeding	50
Bean cleaning and sorting, dipping, packing and wrapping	50
Milling	100
Cream making (mixing, cooking, molding)	50
Gum drops and jellied forms	50
Hand decorating	100
Hard Candy and Toffee Manufacture	
Mixing, cooking and molding	50
Die cutting, sorting and wrapping	100
Canning and preserving	
Initial grading raw materials	100-200
Preparation, preliminary sorting, cutting, pitting, final sorting	100-150

continued over

Operation or Area	Footcandles (Minimum on the task at all times)
Canning	
Continuous belt canning	100
Hand packing	50
Examination and inspection	200
Can unscrambling	70
Labelling and cartoning	30
Auxiliary plant	
Battery rooms, boiler areas, pump bays, cable rooms, control rooms, air-conditioning plant	10-50
Dairy products	
Fluid milk processing	
Bottle sorting and washing	30-50
Can washing	30
Cooling	30
Filling/inspection	100
Laboratories	100
Pasteurizers/separators	30
Inspection	50-1000
Machine shops	50-1000
Flour milling	
Rolling, sifting, purifying	50
Packing	30
Product control	100
Cleaning screens, manlifts, aisleways walkways, bin checking	30
Meat processing and packing	
Storage, lairage	10-50
Slaughtering	30
Cleaning, cutting, grinding, cooking, canning, packing	100
Sugar refining	
Grading	50
Colour inspection	200
Testing	50-200

Source - Adapted from Hall et al (1971).

The iodine value of an edible oil expresses the amount of iodine with which an oil combines as a percentage of its own weight.   Thus when an oil is hydrogenated the fall in I V divided by 127 represents the percentage gain in weight as hydrogen by the oil.   For the purpose of process control it has been found convenient to know the volume of dry hydrogen required to reduce the iodine value by one unit for a standard batch or weight of oil.   The table below shows the theoretical hydrogen requirement and also the hardening plant requirements for hydrogenation factors of 1.05 and 1.10 (hydrogen loss of 5% and 10%).

The Hydrogen Required to Reduce the I V by One Unit

Batch Weight of Oil	Hydrogen requirement	
	0°C, 760 mm Hg	15°C, 760 mm Hg
1000 kg (metric tonne)	0.8835 m³	0.9319 m³
2240 lb (long ton)	31.69 ft³	33.5 ft³
Assuming 5% loss		
1000 kg	0.9277 m³	0.9785 m³
2240 lb	32.27 ft³	35.18 ft³
Assuming 10% loss		
1000 kg	0.9719 m³	1.025 m³
2240 lb	34.86 ft³	36.85 ft³

61

2.17   Selection of Pumps and Compressors

Transportation of Gases

The choice of equipment for the transportation of gases depends upon the flow rate, the differential pressure and the operating pressure demanded.   When the pressure drop is low ($<$ 35 cm H_2O; 0.03 bar), fans are employed.   For moderate differential pressures and high flow rates axial flow compressors are chosen. Centrifugal compressors are used for both high flow rates and high differential pressures.   Steam-jet ejectors are versatile and economic vacuum pumps used extensively in the food industry.

Transportation of Liquids

Normal Operating Range of Process Pumps

Type	Capacity m³/hr	Head m of water
Centrifugal	$0.25-10^3$	10-50
Reciprocating	0.5-500	50-200
Diaphragm	0.05-500	5-60
Rotary, gear, and similar	0.05-500	60-200
Rotary sliding vane	0.25-500	7-70

Source: Coulson, Richardson and Sinnot. Equipment Selection, Specification and Design. Chemical Engineering.

3 The Chemical and Physical Properties of Foods

Food Type	% H_2O	pH	Freezing Point °C	Specific Heat kJ/kg °C A*	B*	Latent Heat kJ/kg	Thermal Conductivity W/m °C
Fruit							
Apple	80-84	3.0-3.3	-2	3.60	1.88	280	0.39-0.42
Banana	75-76	-	-2	3.35	1.76	255	-
Grapefruit	89	-	-2	3.81	1.93	293	0.40-0.45
Orange	87	3.2-3.8	-2	3.77	1.93	288	0.43
Peach	87	3.4-3.6	-2	3.78	1.93	289	0.35-0.45
Pineapple	85	-	-2	3.68	1.88	285	0.35-0.45
Water melon	92	-	-2	4.06	2.01	306	0.56-0.63
Vegetables							
Asparagus	93	5.6-5.7	-1	3.93	2.01	310	-
Beans (green)	89	-	-1	3.81	1.97	297	0.39-0.92
Cabbage	92	5.1-5.3	-1	3.93	1.97	306	-
Carrot	88	-	-1	3.60	1.88	293	0.62-0.67
Corn	76	6.3-6.5	-1	3.35	1.80	251	0.14-0.18
Peas	74	6.1-6.3	-1	3.31	1.76	247	0.32-0.48
Potato	80	5.4-5.8	-2	3.39	1.74	258	0.55
Tomato	95	-	-1	3.98	2.01	310	0.40-0.66
Meat							
Bacon	20	-	-	2.09	1.26	71	-
Beef	75-79	5.5-6.5	-2	3.22	1.67	255	0.43-0.48
Fish	70	6.0	-2	3.18	1.67	276	0.56
Lamb	70-80	-	-2	3.18	1.67	276	0.42-0.45
Pork	60-76	-	-2	3.18	1.67	276	0.44-1.3
Poultry	69-75	6.4-6.6	-2	-	-	-	0.41-0.52
Veal	63	-	-2	2.97	1.67	209	0.44-0.49
Miscellaneous							
Beer	92	4.1-4.3	-2	4.19	2.01	301	0.52-0.64
Bread	32-37	-	-2	2.93	1.42	109-121	-
Butter	15-16	-	-	1.4-2.7	1.2	53.5	0.197
Cereals	12-14	-	-	1.5-1.9	1.2	-	0.13-0.18
Cheese	30-38	4.0-6.5	-2	1.94	1.24	-	
Chocolate	55	-	-1	1.26	2.30	93	-
Cream, 40% fat	73	-	-2	3.52	1.65	-	0.33
Egg	49	-	-3	3.2	1.67	276	0.34-0.62
Ice-cream	58-66	-	-3, -18	3.3	1.88	222	-
Milk	87.5	6.5-6.7	-1	3.9	2.05	289	0.53
Orange juice	89	3.9	-	-	-	-	0.48-0.68
Raisins	24.5	3.6-4.2	-	1.94	-	-	0.55
Sausage	65	-	-3	3.68	2.32	216	0.38-0.43
Salmon	64	6.2-6.4	-3	2.97	1.84	-	0.50-1.3
Yoghurt	-	4.0-4.5	-	-	-	-	0.53-0.67

*A = Above freezing;   B = Below freezing

3.2 pH of Common Foods

3.2.1 pH of a Wide Range of Foods

Food	pH	Food	pH
Lemons	2.3-2.6	Cheese (Port Salut)	5.2-5.5
Vinegar	2.4-2.8	Soups	5.3
Wine	2.8-3.2	Potatoes	5.4-5.8
Preserves	2.8-3.2	Asparagus	5.5
Plums, Currants	2.9-3.2	Pork and Beans	5.5
Olives	3.1	Meats	5.5-6.5
Cucumber	3.1	Spinach	5.5-5.6
Apples	3.0-3.3	Cauliflower	5.6-5.7
Vinegar preserves	3.0-3.3	Cheese (hard)	5.6-6.2
Apple butter	3.3	Green beans	5.7
Grapefruit	3.4	Frankfurters	5.8
Apple sauce	3.8	Fish	6.0
Pineapple juice	3.5	Ham	6.1
Sauerkraut	3.5-4.0	Peas	6.1-6.4
Oranges	3.2-3.8	Sardines	6.1-6.4
Strawberries	3.3-3.4	Salmon	6.2-6.4
Peaches	3.4-3.6	Oysters	6.2-6.5
Cherries	3.4-4.0	Corn beef	6.3
Raisins	3.6-4.2	Lima beans	6.4
Apricots	3.7-3.8	Creamed corn	6.3-6.5
Orange juice	3.9	Poultry	6.4-6.6
Yoghurt/white cheese	4.0-4.5	Mushrooms	6.4
Beer	4.1-4.3	Milk	6.5-6.7
Pumpkin	4.2	Legumes (alkali blanch)	6.5-7.5
Prune juice	3.9	Shrimps	6.8-7.0
Tomato juice	4.3	Corn	6.9
Cheese	4.8	Chicken	7.3
Turnips/Cabbage	5.1-5.3	Soda crackers	7.5
Kidney beans	5.2-5.4		

3.2.2 Typical pH Values of Sugar Confections and their Constituent Raw Materials

Material	pH	Material	pH
Boiled Sweets (Acid)	2.2	Gelatine (lime produced)	5.1
Apple Pulp	2.5	Gloucose syrup	5.2
Lactic Acid (buffered)	3.0	Alginate Jellies	5.3
Pectin Jelly	3.1	Marzipan	6.0
Honey (dependent on source)	3.4-6.0	Cream	6.2
		Cocoa	6.3
Table Jellies	3.8	Milk, evaporated	6.4
Pineapple Pulp	3.8	Liquid Sugars	6.4
Lactose	3.9	Cocoa Butter	6.6
Creams	4.2	Milk Powder	6.6
Gelatine (acid produced)	4.2	Butter	6.6
Gelatine Jellies	4.4	Pure deionised water (neutral)	7.0
Fondant	4.4		
Egg Albumin	4.7	Sodium Alginate (alkaline)	7.7
Gum Tragacanth	5.0		

3.2.3 Post–Mortem pH of Animal Tissues

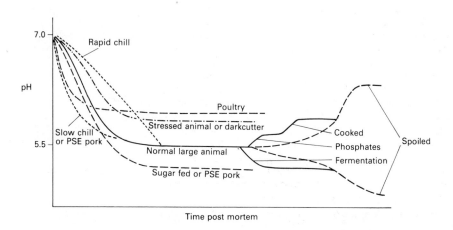

Source : Ockerman. H.W. – Chemistry of Muscle and Major Organs.
In Libby. J.A. (Ed) – Meat Hygiene.
Lea & Febiger. Phiadelphia. 1975

3.2.4   pH Values of Standard Solutions

	pH Values			
Normality	HCl	CH$_3$COOH	NaOH	NH$_3$
1	0.10	2.37	14.05	11.77
0.1	1.07	2.87	13.07	11.27
0.01	2.02	3.37	12.12	10.77
0.001	3.01	3.87	11.13	10.27
0.0001	4.01			

3.2.5   ph Value of Biological Materials

Material	pH Value	Material	pH Value
Blood, normal limits	7.3-7.5	Gastric juice, adult	0.9-1.6
Blood, extreme limits	7.0-7.8	Milk, cows, limits	6.2-7.3
Enzymes activity range of		Milk, human	7.0-7.2
Amylopsin, optimum	7.0	Muscle juice	6.8
Erepsin, optimum	7.8	Plants (extracted juice)	
Invertase, optimum	5.5	Alfalfa tops	5.9
Lipase, pancreatic	7.0-8.0	Carrot	5.2
Maltase, optimum	6.1-6.8	Cucumber	5.1
Pepsin, optimum	1.5-2.4	Peas, field	6.8
Trypsin, optimum	8-9	Potato	6.1
Fruit juices		Rhubarb, stalks	3.4
Apple	3.8	String beans	5.2
Banana	4.6	Saliva	6.2-7.6
Grapefruit	3.0-3.3	Sweat	4.5-7.1
Orange	3.1-4.1	Tears	7.2
Tomato	4.2	Urine, human, limits	4.2-8.2

Source: Peterson, W H, Skinner, J T, and Strong, F M – Elements of Food Biochemistry. Prentice-Hall, Englewood Cliffs, NJ, USA.

3.3   Water Content of a Wide Range of Foodstuffs

3.3.1   Water Content of Vegetables

Commodity	Water Content %	Commodity	Water Content %
Artichokes		Leeks (green)	88.2-92.0
Globe Articokes	83.7	Lentils	12.0
Jerusalem Artichokes	79.5	Lettuce	94.8
Asparagus	93.0	Mushrooms (fresh)	90.1-91.1
Avacados	65.4	Mushrooms (dried)	30.0
Beans		Okra	89.8
Dried	12.5	Onions	87.5
French	90.0	Parsley	65.0-95.0
Green or snap	88.9-90.0	Parsnips	78.6
Lima	65.5-66.5	Peas (dried)	9.5
String	88.9	Peas (green)	74.4-76.0
Beets (topped)	87.6	Peas (air dried)	14.0
Broccoli (sprouting)	89.9	Peppers (sweet)	92.4
Brussel sprouts	84.9	Peppers (chilli, dry)	12.0
Cabbage (late)	92.4	Popcorn (unpopped)	13.5
Cabbage (white, fresh)	90.0-92.0	Potatoes	75.0
Carrots		Potatoes (late crop)	77.8
Bunch	86.0-90.0	Sweet Potatoes	68.5
Boiled	92.0	Pumpkins	90.5
Cauliflower	91.7	Radishes (spring)	93.6
Celeriac	88.3	Radishes	
Celery	93.7	(spring, prepacked)	93.6
Corn (sweet)	73.9	Rutabagas	89.1
Corn (green)	75.5	Sorrel	92.0
Corn (dried)	10.5	Salsify	79.1
Cucumbers	96.1-97.0	Spinach	85.0-92.7
Eggplants	92.7	Squash	88.6-95.0
Endive	93.3	Tomatoes	
Garlic (dry)	74.2	(mature green)	85.0-94.7
Kale	86.6	Tomatoes, (ripe)	94.1
Kohlrabi	90.0	Turnips	90.9

3.3.2 Water Content of Fruits

Commodity	Water Content %	Commodity	Water Content %
Apples	75.0-85.0	Oranges	87.2
Apricots	85.4	Papaya	90.8
Bananas	74.8	Peaches	86.9-90.0
Dates (dried)	20.0	Pears	82.7
Dates (fresh)	78.0	Persimmons	78.2
Figs (dried)	24.0	Pineapples	85.3
Figs (fresh)	78.0	Plums	81.0-85.7
Grapefruit	88.8	Plums and prunes (dry)	28.0-35.0
Lemons	89.3	Pomegranates	85.3
Limes	86.0	Prunes (fresh)	81.0-85.7
Mangoes	81.4	Quinces	85.3
Melons	92.1-92.7	Tangerines	87.3
Nectarines	82.9		

3.3.3 Water Content of Berries

Commodity	Water Content %	Commodity	Water Content %
Blackberries	84.8	Grapes (USA)	81.9
Blueberries	82.3	Grapes (Europe)	81.6
Cherries	83.0	Loganberries	82.9
Cranberries	87.4	Raspberries (black)	80.6
Currants	87.4	Raspberries (red)	84.1
Dewberries	87.4	Strawberries (fresh)	89.9-91.0
Gooseberries	88.9	Strawberries (frozen)	72.0

3.3.4 Water Content of Dairy Products

Commodity	Water Content %	Commodity	Water Content %
Albumen (fermented)	3.0-15.0	Eggs (dried whole)	5.0
Albumen (spray-dried)	6.0	Eggs (dried yolk)	3.0
Butter	15.0-16.0	Eggs (frozen)	73.0
Cheese (non-fat)	50.0	Eggs (shell)	67.0-76.0
Cheeses	30.0-38.0	Ice-cream	58.0-66.0
Cream (sour)	57.0-73.0	Milk (powdered)	12.5
Cream (sweetened)	75.0	Milk (skim)	91.0
Cream cheese	80.0	Milk (whole)	87.5

3.3.5   Water Content of Miscellaneous Foodstuffs

Commodity	Water Content %	Commodity	Water Content %
Bread (white)	44.0-45.0	Nuts (dried)	3.0-10.0
Bread (brown)	48.5	Nuts (whole)	3.0-6.0
Flour	12.0-13.5	Oleo-margarine	15.5
Grains	15.0-20.0	Olives (fresh)	75.2
Macaroni	13.0	Raisins	24.5
Maple sugar	5.0	Rice	10.5-13.5
Maple syrup	36.0	Yeast	70.9

3.3.6   Water Content of Meat

Commodity	Water Content %	Commodity	Water Content %
Bacon	13.0-39.0	Lamb (fresh)	60.0-70.0
Beef (fresh)	62.0-67.0	Lamb (mutton)	90.0
Beef (fat)	50.0	Pork (fresh)	35.0-42.0
Beef (lean)	70.0-76.0	Pork (fresh, fat)	39.0
Beef (dried)	5.0-15.0	Pork (fresh, non-fat)	57.0
Ham (fresh shoulder)	47.0-54.0	Pork (smoked)	57.0
Ham (cured)	40.0-45.0	Sausages (fresh)	65.0

3.3.7 Typical Percentage Moisture Content of Sugar Confectionery, Chocolate and Various Raw Materials

Sugar Confectionery and Chocolate

Sweet	Moisture %	Sweet	Moisture %
Boiled sweets (high)	2.0	Jellies (gelatine)	22.0
Butterscotch	3.5	Jellies (pectin)	22.0
Candied fruit	20.0	Jellies (table)	25.0
Caramels	8.0	Liquorish paste	18.0
Chocolate	1.0	Lozenges	2.5
Creams	14.0	Marshmallow (cast)	18.0
Cream paste	6.0	Marshmallow (grained)	12.0
Fondant	12.0	Nougat	8.0
Fudge	7.0	Tablets (compressed)	1.0
Jellies (agar)	24.0	Turkish delight	20.0

Raw Materials

Component	Moisture %	Component	Moisture %
Agar	16.0	High DE	18.0
Block liquorice juice	18.7	Maltose	16.7
Brown sugar	2.9	Enzyme	16.7
Butter	13.8	Golden syrup	16.7
Candied peel	20.0	Granulated sugar	0.01
Chocolate	1.0	Gum arabic	9.9
Chocolate crumb	1.0	Gum tragacanth	9.9
Citric acid, hydrate	8.3	Honey	18.0
Condensed milk	27.0	Icing sugar	0.01
Cornflower	12.3	Invert sugar	28.0
Dates	24.8	Lactose	0.1
Dextrose hydrate	9.1	Milk powder	22.9
Fruit pulp	39.8	Nuts	2.0
Gelatine	12.3	Sorbitol	30.0
Glucose syrup		Soya flour	7.4
Low DE	19.4	Starch	10.7
Regular	18.7	Wheat flour	13.8

3.4 Viscosity of Food Liquids

3.4.1 Variation of the Viscosity of Water with Temperature

Temperature °C	Viscosity centipoises	Temperature °C	Viscosity centipoises
0	1.7921	51	0.5404
1	1.7313	52	0.5315
2	1.6728	53	0.5229
3	1.6191	54	0.5146
4	1.5674	55	0.5064
5	1.5188	56	0.4985
6	1.4728	57	0.4907
7	1.4284	58	0.4832
8	1.3860	59	0.4759
9	1.3462	60	0.4688
10	1.3077	61	0.4618
11	1.2713	62	0.4550
12	1.2363	63	0.4483
13	1.2028	64	0.4418
14	1.1709	65	0.4355
15	1.1404	66	0.4293
16	1.1111	67	0.4233
17	1.0828	68	0.4174
18	1.0559	69	0.4117
19	1.0299	70	0.4061
20	1.0050	71	0.4006
20	1.0000	72	0.3952
21	0.9810	73	0.3900
22	0.9579	74	0.3849
23	0.9358	75	0.3799
24	0.9142	76	0.3750
25	0.8937	77	0.3702
26	0.8737	78	0.3655
27	0.8545	79	0.3610
28	0.8360	80	0.3565
29	0.8180	81	0.3521
30	0.8007	82	0.3478
31	0.7840	83	0.3436
32	0.7679	84	0.3395
33	0.7523	85	0.3355
34	0.7371	86	0.3315
35	0.7225	87	0.3276
36	0.7085	88	0.3239
37	0.6947	89	0.3202
38	0.6814	90	0.3165
39	0.6685	91	0.3130
40	0.6560	92	0.3095
41	0.6439	93	0.3060
42	0.6321	94	0.3027
43	0.6207	95	0.2994
44	0.6097	96	0.2962

3.4.2 Density and Viscosity of Aqueous Solutions

Material	Concentration %	Temp ^{0}C	Density kg/m^3	Viscosity Ns/m^2 x 10^3
Acetic Acid	-	20	1050	1.2
Calcium Chloride	24	-23	1238	12.5
	25	0	-	4.55
	25	20	-	2.4
	25	40	-	1.28
	25	60	-	0.72
Sodium Chloride	22	2	1240	2.7
	22	0	1190	6.1
Sucrose	20	20	1070	1.92
	20	80	-	0.59
	60	20	-	60.2
	60	80	-	5.4
	60	95	-	3.7
Sulphuric Acid	-	20	1830	25.0

3.4.3 Density and Viscosity of Milk and Cream

Material	Concentration	Temp ^{0}C	Density kg/m^3	Viscosity Ns/m^2 x 10^3
Whole milk	-	20	1030	2.12
	-	0	1035	4.28
	-	20	1030	2.12
	-	70	1012	0.7
Skimmed milk	-	25	1040	1.4
Cream	20% fat	3	1010	6.2
	30% fat	3	1000	13.8

3.4.4 Density and Viscosity of Miscellaneous Food Liquids

Material	Temperature ^{0}C	Density kg/m^3	Viscosity Ns/m^2 x 10^3
Ammonia	-15	660	0.25
	27	600	0.21
Beer	0	1000	1.3
Castor Oil	10	969	2420
	20		986
	40		231
Ethanol	20	790	1.2
Freon 12	-15	1440	0.33
	27	1300	0.26
Honey	25	1400	6000
Methyl Alcohol	0	810	0.813
	20		0.591
Molasses	21	1430	6600
	37.8	1380	1872
	49	1310	920
	66	1160	374

3.4.5 The Viscosity and Composition of Types of Glucose Syrup

Type	Low DE	Low DE	Regular DE	Inter-mediate DE	High DE	High Maltose
Degree Baumè	41.2	43.2	43.2	43.2	43.2	43.2
Total Solids %	75.97	80.67	80.67	81.55	82.03	80.67
Dextrose Equivalent %	26	38	42	55	64	42
Ash	0.3	0.3	0.3	0.3	0.3	0.3
Monosaccharides %	8.0	15.0	19.3	30.8	37.0	5.9
Disaccharides (Maltose)	7.5	12.5	14.3	18.1	31.5	44.4
Trisaccharides	7.5	11.0	11.8	13.2	11.0	12.7
Tetrasaccharides	7.0	9.0	10.0	9.5	5.0	3.3
Pentasaccharides	6.5	8.0	8.4	7.2	4.0	1.3
Hexasaccharides	5.0	7.0	6.6	5.1	3.0	1.5
Heptasaccharides	4.5	5.0	5.6	4.2	2.0	1.0
Octa-saccharides and high mol weight sugars	54.0	32.5	24.0	11.9	6.9	29.4
Viscosity, Cp, at 16°C (60°F) $\times 10^6$	5.0	3.6	3.4	2.2	1.3	3.4
Processing	acid conv	acid conv	acid conv	acid or enzyme conv	enzyme conv	enzyme conv

NB   DE = Dextrose equivalent.

3.5 Boiling Point of Sucrose (Cane and Beet Sugar) Solutions

3.5.1 Boiling Point versus Concentration

Sucrose Concentration %	Boiling Point °C	°F
40	101.4	214.5
50	102	215.5
60	103	217.5
70	105.5	222
75	108	227
80	111	232
85	116	241
90	122	252
95	130	266

3.5.2 Effect of Boiling Under Vacuum

Total Solids Value (appropriate %)	Open Boil °C	°F	Vacuum Cooking °C	°F	lb/in²
96	143.4	290	129.5	265	25
97	150	302	135	275	27
98	160.1	320	140.6	285	28

3.6   Food Rheological Data

Product	Temp ^{0}C	Conc % TS	Consistency Pa s^n	Flow behaviour Index (n)	Method	Reference
Apple Juice	27	20^{0}Brix	0.0021	1.0	Cap tube	1
Apple Juice	27	60^{0}Brix	0.03	1.0	Cap tube	1
Apple Sauce	24	unknown	0.66	0.408	Cap tube	2
Apple Sauce	25	31.7	22.0	0.4	Coax cyl	3
Apple Sauce	27	11.6	12.7	0.28	Cap tube	1
Apricot Conc	25	26	67.0	0.3	Coax cyl	3
Apricot Puree	21	17.7	5.4	0.29	Coax cyl	4
Apricot Puree	25	19	20.0	0.3	Coax cyl	4
Apricot Puree	27	13.8	7.2	0.41	Cap tube	1
Banana Puree	20	unknown	6.89	0.46	Cap tube	2
Banana Puree	24	unknown	10.7	0.333	Cap tube	2
Banana Puree	42	unknown	5.26	0.486	Cap tube	2
Banana Puree	49	unknown	4.15	0.478	Cap tube	2
Corn Syrup	27	48.4	0.053	1.0	Coax cyl	4
Cream (20%fat)	3		0.0062	1.0	unknown	5
Cream (30%fat)	3		0.0138	1.0	unknown	5
Grape Juice	27	20^{0}Brix	0.0025	1.0	Cap tube	1
Grape Juice	27	60^{0}Brix	0.11	1.0	Cap Tube	1
Honey	24	normal	5.6-6.2	1.0	Cap tube	2
Olive Oil	20	normal	0.084	1.0	unknown	5
Peach Puree	27	10.0	0.94-4.5	.34-.44	Coax cyl	6
Pear Puree	27	14.6	5.3	0.38	Cap tube	1

Product	Temp °C	Conc % TS	Consist-ency Pa s^n	Flow behav-iour Index (n)	Method	Reference
Pear Puree	27	15.2	4.25	0.35	Coax cyl	4
Pear Puree	32	18.31	2.25	0.486	Coax cyl	6
Pear Puree	32	45.75	35.5	0.479	Coax cyl	6
Skim Milk	25	normal	0.0014	1.0	unknown	5
Soy Bean Oil	30	normal	0.04	1.0	unknown	5
Tomato Conc	32	5.8	0.223	0.59	Coax cyl	7
Tomato Conc	32	30	18.7	0.4	Coax cyl	7
Whole Milk	20	normal	0.0212	1.0	unknown	5

NB Cap tube = capillary tube, Coax cyl = coaxial cylinder

References

1   Saravacos 1968
2   Charm 1978
3   Watson 1968
4   Harper 1960
5   Mohsenin 1970
6   Harper & Lebermann 1964
7   Harper & El Sahrigi

3.7   Density of Solid Food Commodities

Bulk Density and Porosity

Bulk density is the mass of the particles that occupies unit volume of the container. Porosity is the fraction of the container volume not occupied by solid material.

$$\text{Total porosity} = 1 - \frac{\text{bulk density}}{\text{solid density}}$$

Since powders are compressible their bulk density is usually given with an additional specifier; (as poured), (after vibration) or (after compression).

3.7.1   Approximate Bulk Density and Moisture of Various Powders

Food Powder	Bulk Density kg/m³	Moisture Content %
Baby-food formula	400	2.5
Cocoa	480	3-5
Coffee (ground, roasted)	330	7
Coffee (instant)	330	2.5
Coffee (creamer)	470	3
Cornmeal	660	12
Cornstarch	560	12
Egg (whole)	340	2-4
Gelatin (ground)	680	12
Microcrystalline cellulose	680	6
Milk	610	2-4
Oatmeal	430	8
Onion (powdered)	510	1-4
Salt (granulated)	960	0.2
Salt (powdered)	950	0.2
Soy protein (precipitated)	280	2-3
Sugar (granulated)	800	0.5
Sugar (powdered)	480	0.5
Wheat flour	480	12
Whey	560	4.5

3.7.2 Solid Density of Food Particles

Food Material	Solid Density kg/m^3
Cellulose	1270-1610
Citric Acid	1540
Fat	900-950
Glucose	1560
Protein (globular)	1400
Salt	2160
Starch	1500
Sucrose	1590

NB Data from Peleg.

3.8 Physical Characteristics of Food Powders

3.8.1 Typical Screen Analysis of Granulated Sugar

Tyler Screen	US % Retained	Medium Gran	Fine Gran	Extra Fine Gran	Standard Powdered	Fondant and Icing
10 mesh	10 mesh	5.6				
14 mesh	16 mesh	59.0				
20 mesh	20 mesh	27.4				
28 mesh	30 mesh	7.4	4.3	0.1		
35 mesh	40 mesh	0.4	74.5	13.8		
48 mesh	50 mesh	–	18.6	40.2		
80 mesh	80 mesh	–	2.3	40.6		
100 mesh	100 mesh				0.3	
150 mesh	140 mesh				1.8	
200 mesh					6.6	
270 mesh					8.2	
325 mesh					10.8	
Thro' last sieve		0.2	0.3	5.0	72.3	99.0

NB The extremely fine grain size of fondant and icing sugar make regular screen analysis inpractical. The average particle size of fondant and icing sugar is of the order of 20μ (0.0008 ins).

3.8.2   Typical Particle Size Data on Cake Mixes

Size Range	Cake Flour	Enriched Sponge (cake premix)	Chocolate Cake (cake premix)
Microns	% oversize	% oversize	% oversize
2.0	–	–	98.2
2.5	99.2	98.9	94.9
3.2	97.5	97.1	90.0
4.0	94.4	93.7	83.0
5.0	89.6	88.5	74.7
6.4	84.0	83.3	65.9
8.0	78.8	78.6	58.5
10.1	74.1	73.8	52.1
12.7	66.0	66.2	44.5
16.0	48.7	51.6	31.9
20.2	27.4	33.3	15.9
25.4	13.6	20.7	6.3
32.0	9.2	16.4	1.8
40.3	7.3	13.2	–
Average Particle Size	15.8	16.4	10.5

3.8.3   Typical Screen Analysis of a Seasoning Mixture

Material	Weight %
Colour	3
Colour retainer	6
Coriander	2
Dextrose	8
Fine rusk	9
Ginger	1
Nutmeg	3
Pepper	8
Polyphosphate	6
Preservative	4
Salt	50

+ 10 mesh	nil
+ 20 mesh	42%
+ 40 mesh	34%
- 40 mesh	24%

3.8.4   Evaluation of the Flow Properties of Food Powders

One of the standard test methods used to evaluate the flow properties of particulate solids mixtures involves the computation of the 'Hausner Ratio'. The Hausner Ratio of a powder is defined as the ratio of its 'Loose Bulk Density', to its 'Tapped Bulk Density', and is considered to represent a measure of the flowability of the powder.

$$\text{Hausner Ratio} \quad \frac{\text{Tapped Density}}{\text{Loose Density}} \qquad \frac{\text{Loose Volume}}{\text{Tapped Volume}}$$

Hausner Ratio	Powder Flowability
1.0-1.1	free flowing
1.1-1.25	medium flowing
1.25-1.4	difficult
>1.4	very difficult

In order to determine the loose volume the test material is inverted several times in a graduated measuring cylinder and the average loose volume is recorded.

A similar technique used to evaluate the flow properties of food powders involves the computation of the 'flowability index', using the 'Novadel Tap Test'.   To determine the flowability index the measuring cylinder filled with the test material is placed upon the 'Englesman Tapping Machine', and the programmer set to 70 taps. At the end of the tapping routine the volume decrease is expressed as a percentage.

Volume Decrease	Flowability
<10%	free flowing
10-20%	medium-sticky
20-35%	difficult
>35%	very difficult

A graphical combination of the two methods can then be used to give a more reliable assessment of the powder flow properties. This technique and some typical Hausner Ratio data   are presented on p.84.

Comparison & Combination of Flowability Tests

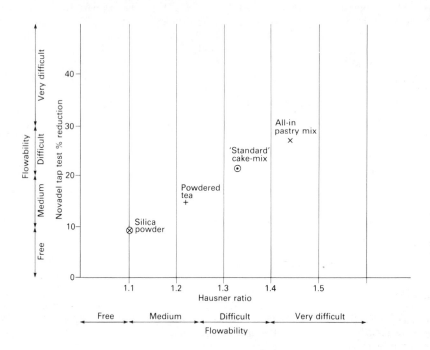

Typical Hausner Ratio and Novadel Tap-Test Results

Material	Tapped Density	Novadel Tap Test	Hausner Ratio
'All-in Pastry Mix'	–	27	1.43
Calcium Phosphate	1.0	12.5	1.72
Defatted Soya Flour	0.487	24	1.85
Glyceryl Monostearate	0.551	21	1.67
Magnesium Oxide	2.041	12	1.2
Malted Flour	0.656	20	1.33
Methyl Cellulose	0.546	9	1.18
'Novadelox' (benzoyl peroxide)	1.436	11	1.51
Powdered Tea	0.732	14	1.22
'Standard Cake-Mix'	–	22	1.33
Silica Powder (control)	–	9	1.10
Vitamin C Mix	0.766	12	1.15
Vitamin Mix (riboflavin)	0.654	20	1.35

3.9 Strength and Mechanical Properties of Foods

3.9.1 Particle Hardness

The characteristic of particle hardness in a bulk material is of primary interest in relation to its potential abrasiveness, how easily it cracks, crumbles or reduces to smaller particles. No known method of evaluating material is universally applicable to all bulk materials. In 1822 Mohs set up the relative hardness table shown below which, although it is purely qualitative, it is widely used to compare the hardness of minerals, ores and rocks. Only a limited amount of data is available regarding the hardness of food particles such as cereals, nuts, toffee or candy.

MOHS Hardness Scale

1.0	Talc	6.0	Orthoclase
2.0	Gypsum	6.0	Cement Clinker
2.5	Fingernail		Feldspar, Rutile
3.0	Calcite		Sand
3.0	Copper coin	7.0	Quartz
	Limestone	7.0	Iron Ore Sinter
	Bauxite		Silica Sand
4.0	Fluorite	7.5	Zircon
4.0	Cementrock	8.0	Topaz
	Taconite Pellets	8.5	Chrysoberyl
5.0	Apartite	9.0	Sapphire
5.0	Mill Scale	9.0	Aluminium Oxide
5.5	Knife blade	9.5	Carborundum
	Glasses	10.0	Diamond

3.9.2 Measurement of Powder Cohesion

The flow function of a cohesive food powder may be determined by means of the UCT technique developed at Bradford University by Williams, Birks and Bhattacharya, in which the powder is first compacted in a split cylindrical mould after which the mould is carefully dismantled and the powder compact collapsed by the successive addition of weights.

Using the cylindrical split cell, (diagram overleaf) and the standard compacting load of 10kg;

Good Flowing	$w < 1$ kg
Moderate Flowing	1 kg $< w < 2$ kg
Cohesive	2 kg $< w < 5$ kg
Very Cohesive	5 kg $< w$

where w is the total weight causing the compact to fail.

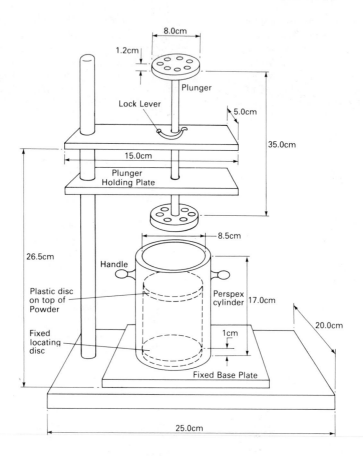

UCT Apparatus

For routine quality control purposes the yield weight alone may be used to indicate the flow properties of a food powder.

Typical Test Results Using The UCT Equipment (Catering Cake Mix)

	Compaction Load			Yield	
kg	lbs	lbs/in^2	kN/m^2	lbs/in^2	kN/m^2
0.91	2	0.344	2.37	0.123	0.849
1.36	3	0.453	3.13	0.123	0.849
1.82	4	0.564	3.89	0.151	1.041
2.27	5	0.674	4.65	0.178	1.231
2.72	6	0.784	5.41	0.233	1.611
3.18	7	0.894	6.17	0.261	1.801
3.63	8	1.004	6.93	0.261	1.801
4.09	9	1.115	7.69	0.344	2.374
4.54	10	1.225	8.45	0.371	2.561

3.9.3   Measurement of The Mechanical Properties of Foods

A number of publications are available that describe the instrumentation used to quantify those mechanical properties of food relating to their rheological and textural characteristics.   The current trend   is to use a universal test machine eg the 'Instron' for the drive mechanism, sensory element, data record and readout, and to have available a variety of probes and attachments to suit almost any food application.

The Characteristic Features of Texture Testing Instruments

Basic Elements

Probe   Flat plunger, puncture element, mechanical tooth, penetrating cone, cutting blade, saw, tensile grips, extrusion element, shear cell.

Drive   Hydraulic system, variable drive electric motor.

Sensing   Strain gauge, load cell.

Readout   Oscilloscope, X-Y recorder, microprocessor.

Classification of Texture Testing Instruments According to Measured Variable

Method	Measured Variable	Units (dimensional)	Examples
Force measuring	Force (F)	ML/T^2	Tenderometer
Distance measure	Distance	L	Penetrometer
	Area	L^2	Grawemeyer Consistometer
	Volume	L^3	Seed Displacement
Time measure	Time	T	Oswald Viscometer
Energy measure	Work (FxL)	ML^2/T^2	Farinograph
Ratio measure	F, L or T	none	Cohesion Evaluation
Multiple measuring	F, L and T F x L	ML/T^2	Texturometer
Multiple variable	F, L or T	–	Dorometer
Chemical analysis	Concentration	%, ppm	Insoluble solids content

3.10.1   Composition and Analytical Characteristics of Fats and Oil Products
          in the USA

	Household Shortening		Commercial Shortening		Salad Oil
	Vegetable Fat	Meat/ Vegetable Fat	Vegetable Fat	Meat/ Vegetable Fat	Cotton- seed Oil
Composition %					
Oleic acid	53-75	37-57	40-65	42-79	17-36
Linoleic acid	3-74	6-13	3-13	3-13	42-55
Linolenic acid	0-0.5	0-0.6	0-0.7	0-0.8	0-0.7
Arachidonic acid	0	0-0.5	0	0-0.5	0
Total saturated acids	16-31	30-50	15-40	28-40	18-30
Analytical Characteristics					
Iodine value	70-81	57-74	65-90	55-67	107-117
Melting Pt (^{0}F)	108-125	114-129	103-124	110-125	-
Solids index at (70^{0}F)	15-30	16-28	16-26	19-30	-
Solids index at (90^{0}F)	10-20	10-22	7-21	7-21	-

	Beef Fat	Butter Fat	Coco Butter	Coconut Oil
Composition %				
Oleic acid	35-45	30-32	34-38	6-9
Linoleic acid	0.5-3	1-2.5	3-3.5	1-4
Linolenic acid	0.2-0.6	0.2-0.5	0.1-0.2	0-0.1
Arachidonic acid	0.05-0.2	0.2-0.4	-	-
Total saturated acids	45-58	63-68	57-61	86-91
Analytical Characteristics				
Iodine value	38-44	30-40	37-44	8-15
Melting Point (^{0}F)	116-121	97-100	86-95	79-82
Solids index (70^{0}F)	23-30	11-13	47-49	19-27
Solids index (90^{0}F)	18-24	2.5-4	0	0

continued over

	Corn Oil	Cottonseed Oil	Lard	Olive Oil
Composition %				
Oleic acid	25–37	17–37	47–83	62–83
Linoleic acid	50–56	44–55	7–13	8–15
Linolenic acid	0.1–0.7	0–0.6	0.2–1.4	0.5–0.7
Arachidonic acid	–	–	0.2–0.4	–
Total Saturated acids	9–15	17–31	29–37	9–22
Analytical Characteristics				
Iodine value	122–125	103–112	63–69	76–88
Melting Point (^{0}F)	–	–	99–112	–
Solids index (70^{0}F)	–	–	17–21	–
Solids index (90^{0}F)	–	–	4–6	–

	Peanut Oil	Soybean Oil	Palm Oil	Palm Kernel Oil	Rape seed Oil	Salflower Oil
Composition %						
Oleic acid	30–58	16–47	34–56	14	59–62	10–23
Linoleic acid	21–37	39–53	10–11	2–3	15	69–78
Linolenic acid	0–0.5	4–9	0.1–0.4	–	9–10	0.2
Arachidonic acid	–	–	–	–	–	–
Total saturated acids	16–26	5–24	34–50	84	14–16	5–13
Analytical Characteristics						
Iodine value	90–99	125–130	51–58	16–18	103–109	141–150
Melting Point ^{0}F	–	–	103–105	84–66	–	–
Solids index 70^{0}F	–	–	11–11	31–33	–	–
Solids index 90^{0}F	–	–	6–8	–	–	–

3.10.2   Fatty Acid Composition of Common Fats and Oils

Acid Commonly referred to	GC Common Name	Babassu	Butter Fat	Cocoa Butter	Coconut	Corn	Cotton-seed	Lard
Caprylic	C8.0	7	1.5	-	8	-	-	-
Capric	C10.0	5	3	-	7	-	0.1	-
Lauric	C12.0	45	4	-	48.2	-	0.1	0.1
Myristic	C14.0	15	12	0.5	18	0.2	0.9	1
Palmitic	C16.0	9	25	25	8.5	12	23.5	23
Stearic	C18.0	3	9	35	2.3	2.2	2.5	9
Oleic	C18.1	13	-	37.5	6	27	18	46
Linoleic	C18.2	2	-	2	2	57	54	14
Arachidic	C20.0	0.1	1	-	-	0.3	0.3	0.2
Linolenic	C18.3	-	-	-	-	-	-	-
Gadoleic	C20.1	-	-	-	1	0.3	1	-
Behenic	C22.0	-	-	-	-	-	-	Tr
Lignoceric	C24.0	-	-	-	-	-	-	-
Iodine No Typical		16	30	40	9	125	110	73
Iodine No (range)		15-19	25-35	35-43	8-12	120-128	105-116	65-80
Sap Value (range)		247-250	216-240	190-200	254-262	189-193	189-198	190-
Wiley Melting Pt °F		79	82-95	79-99	76	-	-	88-110

Acid Commonly referred to	Palm Oil	Palm Kernel Oil	Peanut Oil	Rape seed Oil	Rice Bran Oil	Soybean Oil	Sunflower Oil
Caprylic	-	4	-	-	-	-	-
Capric	-	4	-	-	-	-	-
Lauric	-	50	0.2	-	-	-	-
Myristic	1	16	0.1	-	0.5	-	-
Palmitic	46	8	11	3	17	11	8
Stearic	4	2.5	3	1.5	2.5	4	3
Oleic	37	12	46	32	46	25	20
Linoleic	10	3	31	19	32	50	67.8
Arachidic	0.4	0.1	1.5	-	0.5	0.4	0.5
Linolenic	0.3	0.1	-	10	-	-	-
Gadoleic	-	-	-	-	-	-	-
Behenic	-	-	3.3	0.5	-	0.3	0.2
Lignoceric	-	-	1.3	-	-	-	-
Iodine No Typical	50	17	100	101	145	130	40
Iodine No Range	45-55	16-20	90-110	95-108	135-150	125-140	35-45
Sap Value (range)	196-200	244-255	170-180	183-194	188-192	188-194	196-200
Wiley Melting Point °F	104-110	80	-	-	-	-	-

3.10.3   A Compendium of the Physical and Chemical Properties of Fats and Oils

Fat or Oil	Melting Point	Specific Gravity*	Refractive Index	Iodine Value	Saponification No
Land Animals					
Butterfat	32.2	0.911_{40}	1.4548	36.1	227
Lard oil	[30.5]	0.919_{15}	1.4615	58.6	198.5
Tallow, beef	49.5	–	–	–	197
Tallow, mutton	[42.0]	0.945_{25}	1.4565	40	194
Marine Animals					
Cod-liver oil	–	0.925_{25}	1.481_{25}	165	186
Herring oil	–	0.900_{60}	1.4610_{60}	140	192
Menhaden oil	–	0.903_{60}	1.4645_{60}	170	191
Sardine oil	–	0.905_{60}	1.4660_{60}	185	193
Sperm oil, body	–	–	–	76–88	122–130
Sperm oil, head	–	–	–	70	140–144
Whale oil	–	0.892_{60}	1.460_{60}	120	195
Plants					
Babassu oil	22–26	0.893_{60}	1.443_{60}	15.5	247
Castor oil	[-18]	0.961_{15}	1.4770	85.5	180.3
Cocoa butter	34.1	0.964_{15}	1.4568	36.5	195
Coconut oil	25.1	0.924_{15}	1.4493	10.4	257
Corn oil	[-20]	0.922_{15}	1.4734	122.6	190
Cottonseed oil	[-1.0]	0.917_{25}	1.4735	105.7	194.3
Olive oil	[-6.0]	0.918_{15}	1.4679	81.1	192
Palm oil	35.0	0.915_{15}	1.4578	54.2	199.1
Palm kernel oil	24.1	0.923_{15}	1.4569	37.0	250
Peanut oil	[3.0]	0.914_{15}	1.4691	93.4	192.1
Rapeseed oil	[-10]	0.915_{15}	1.4706	98.6	174.7
Safflower oil	–	0.900_{60}	1.462_{60}	145	192
Soybean oil	[-16]	0.927_{15}	1.4729	130	190.6
Sunflower seed oil	[-17.0]	0.923_{15}	1.4694	125.5	188.7
Wheat-germ oil	–	0.929_{25}	1.4745	125	174.5

* Specific Gravity at stated temperature (suffix)

3.10.4 Viscosities of Fats and Oils

Oil	Specific	Kinematic Viscosity		Saybolt Viscosity	
		100°F (37.8°C)	210°F (99°C)	100°F (37.8°C)	210°F (99°C)
Almond	0.9188	43.20	8.74	201	54.0
Olive	0.9158	46.68	9.09	216	55.2
Rapeseed	0.9114	50.64	10.32	234	59.4
Mustard	0.9237	45.13	9.46	209	56.9
Cottonseed	0.9187	35.88	8.39	181	52.7
Soybean	0.9228	28.49	7.60	134	50.1
Sunflower	0.9207	33.31	7.68	156	50.3
Coconut	0.9226	29.79	6.06	140	45.2
Palm kernel	0.9190	30.92	6.50	145	46.5
Lard	0.9138	44.41	8.81	206	54.2
Sardine	0.9384	27.86	7.06	131	48.3
Cod liver	0.9138	32.79	7.80	153	50.7

3.10.5 Titres of Common Fats and Oils

Fat or Oil	Titre Point °C	Fat or Oil	Titre Point °C
Babassu	22-23	Palm Kernel	20-28
Borneo tallow	51-53	Peanut	26-32
Butterfat	33-38	Rape	11-15
Cocao butter	45-50	Rice bran	26-28
Coconut	20-24	Safflower	15-18
Cod liver	18-24	Sardine	27-28
Corn	14-20	Sesame	20-25
Cottonseed	30-37	Soybean	21-23
Hempseed	14-17	Sperm	8-14
Horse fat	34-38	Sunflower	16-20
Kapok	27-32	Tallow beef	40-47
Lard	32-43	Tallow mutton	43-48
Linseed	19-21	Teaseed	13-18
Mustard (black)	6-8	Tung	36-37
Mustard (white)	8-10	Walnut	14-16
Olive	17-26	Whale	22-24
Palm	40-47	Wool fat	38-40

Source: Mahlenbacker C V, The Analysis of Fats and Oils, Garrard Press, Champaign, Illinois.

3.10.6   Smoke, Flash and Fire Point of Fats and Oils

The smoke, flash and fire points of fats and oils are a measure of thermal stability when heated in air.

The smoke point is the temperature at which smoke is first detected when the test is carried out in a standard apparatus (B.S.I. 19776b; AOCS official methods; 1973c) designed such that the relevant parts are draught-free and with a special illumination.   The temperature at which the material smokes freely is usually several degrees higher than at which it is first detected.

The flash point is the temperature at which volatile products are evolved at such a rate as to render them capable of being ignited but not of supporting combustion. This test is carried out in the 'Pensky-Martens' closed cup apparatus (AOCS official methods, 1973d).

The fire point is the temperature at which the production of volatile products is sufficient to support continuous combustion.

Since fatty acids, mono- and diglycerides are less stable than triglycerides, the smoke point of oils will depend to a marked extent upon the level of these compounds contained within them.   The figure below   illustrates   the relationship between smoke, flash and fire points and the free fatty acid content of fats and oils.

Relationship between smoke, flash and fire points and the free fatty acid content of fats and oils

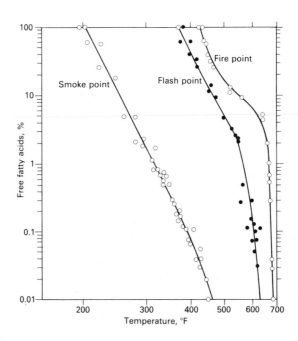

3.10.7 Composition of Butter and Butter Products

Product	% Fat	% H_2O	% Salt	% Curd
Butterfat/ vegetable fat blend	82.5	15.0	1.5	1.0
Butter oil	99.0	1.0	–	–
Dry milkfat	99.9	0.1	–	–
Margarine	80.5	15.4	2.4	1.65
Salted butter	80.5	15.8	2.4	0.9
Unsalted butter	81.0	18.05	–	0.95

Source: Arbuckle W S 1973, Dairy Products in Quality Control for the Food Industry, Vol 2 3rd Edit, A Kramer and B A Twigg (Editors), AVI Publishing Co, Westport, Conn.

3.10.8 Typical Margarine Formulations

Puff Pastry Margarine	%	Margarine rich in Essential Fatty Acids	%
Premier jus	25	Coconut oil/PKO	30
Hardened Palm oil	25	Palm oil	10
Hardened Groundnut oil	10	Palm kernel oil	15
Liquid oil	40	Hard Palm oil	10
		Hard Sunflower	35

Margarine rich in Poly-unsaturated Fatty Acids	%	Interesterified Margarine Blend	%
Liquid Sunflower oil	88	Liquid Sunflower	20
Hardened PKO	6	Hardened Sunflower (33°C)	40
Hard Palm	6	Hardened Sunflower (42°C)	20
		Liquid Sunflower	20

Source: Stuyvenberg J H, Margarine 1969, Liverpool University Press, UK.

3.10.9   Composition and Physical Properties of Milk

Property	Range of Values
Acidity %	0.16 ± 0.02
Boiling point ^{0}C	100.17
Electrical conductivity (mho)	$45-48 \times 10^{-4}$
Freezing point ^{0}C	-0.55
pH	6.6 ± 0.2
Specific gravity	1.032 ± 0.004
Specific heat 0^0C	3.852 kJ/kg ^{0}C
Specific heat 15^0C	3.927 kJ/kg ^{0}C
Specific heat 40^0C	3.894 kJ/kg ^{0}C
Surface tension (dynes)	55.3
Viscosity (centipoisse)	1.6314

Component	Cow	Human	Goat	Sheep
Albumen %	0.5	0.7	0.7	1.3
Ash %	0.7	0.21	0.73	0.93
Casein %	2.9	0.9	2.8	3.6
Fat %	4.0	3.7	4.25	7.92
Lactose %	4.9	7.0	4.2	4.8
Protein (total)	3.5	1.6	3.52	5.2
Specific Gravity	1.032	1.029	1.035	1.034
Total Solids %	13.1	12.5	13.0	19.29

Adapted from Arbuckle W S, Dairy Products, Quality Control for the Food Industry.

3.10.10   Composition of Dairy Products

Material	Protein	Mineral	Lactose	Fat
Butter	0.6	0.2	0.4	80.5
Casein (commercial)	88.5	3.8	-	0.2
Cheese (cottage)	19.2	1.7	4.3	0.8
Cheese (fat, min, all types)	24.5	3.4	1.8	32.0
Cheese (partially defatted)	39.0	5.4	2.8	15.0
Condensed (sweetened)	7.5	1.5	10.5	8.5
Condensed buttermilk	10.6	3.3	13.0	2.0
Condensed skim milk	11.0	2.6	13.5	0.2
Cream	2.9	0.6	4.0	20.0
Cultured buttermilk and chocolate drinks	3.5	0.7	4.6	2.0
Dry buttermilk	32.0	10.0	46.0	5.0
Dry buttermilk solids	34.0	8.0	48.0	5.8
Dry cream	13.4	2.9	18.0	65.0
Dry ice cream	10.5	2.3	15.0	27.0
Dry skim milk	35.0	8.2	51.0	0.8
Dry whey	13.0	9.5	71.0	0.5
Dry whey solids	13.0	8.0	73.0	1.0
Dry whole milk	26.5	6.0	38.5	26.75
Evaporated milk	7.0	1.5	9.9	7.9
Frozen desserts	1.0	0.2	1.3	1.5
Ice cream and ice cream mix	3.8	0.9	5.3	12.0
Lactose	0	0	99.5	0
Liquid separated milk	3.3	0.8	4.8	0.06
Liquid whey	0.8	0.6	4.5	0.05
Malted milk	7.3	1.6	9.9	8.25
Non-fat dry milk solids	36.9	8.15	50.75	0.88
Partially defatted dry milk solids	31.2	7.0	45.3	13.8
Semi-solid buttermilk	10.6	3.3	13.0	2.0
Separated condensed (plain)	7.3	1.6	10.8	0.3
Separated condensed (sweet)	8.8	2.0	12.7	0.5
Whole milk	3.3	0.7	4.5	3.75

Source: Cook H L and Day G H, The Dry Milk Industry, American Dry Milk
    Institute, Chicago 1967.

3.11   Dilatations, SFI and NMR Data on Oils and Fats

The technique for observing changes in density or volume with varying temperatures and time is known as dilatometry, and the instrument used is known as a dilatometer. Dilatometry has become one of the few direct practical methods by which the plastic range and consistency of commercial oil and fat blends may be evaluated and controlled.

Because solidified oils and fats often consist of a mixture of solids and liquids, their density is not comparable to the density of either liquid oil or solid fat. The density of a commercial fat blend depends largely upon the relative proportions of the two phases, which may change rapidly with temperature.

In recent years solids content measurement using pulse NMR has replaced dilatation measurement for routine process control. However, the relationship between dilatation measurements and solids content as determined by NMR, is non−linear.

Conversion of NMR Solids to Dilatations.

NMR Solids determined by "Bruker"Minispec Pc 20. Dilatations determined by British Standards Method.

For solids having slip melting points:

Temperature ^{0}C	Up to 35^{0}C	35^{0}C to 45^{0}C	From 46^{0}C to 55^{0}C
0	16.7	17.4	18.5
20	20.9	20.9	21.1
25	22.7	23.1	22.0
30	24.6	25.6	24.1
35	27.0	29.6	26.1
40	–	34.4	30.2
45	–	43.4	36.5
50	–	–	44.7

NB   The above conversion factors represent the value by which 1% solids as determined by NMR may be converted to dilatations (at T^{0}C).

eg   A fat of slip melting point 38^{0}C has 50% solids @ 0^{0}C, and 35% solids @ 20^{0}C.

To convert to dilatations:

@ 0^{0}C   50 x 17.4 = 870
@ 20^{0}C   35 x 20.9 = 731

Hence at 0^{0}C D = 870 and at 20^{0}C D = 731.

Conversion of SFI Units to Dilatation Units

Although there is no hard and fast relationship between SFI units and Dilatation units, the following conversion technique may be employed as a rough guide:

1 SFI unit ≡ 25 Dilatation units (up to 30 °C)

1 SFI unit ≡ 18–20 Dilatation units (above 30 °C)

3.12 Density and S.G. of Aqueous Solutions

The Variation of the Specific Gravity of Phosphoric Acid with Temperature and Concentration

°C	2%	6%	14%	20%	26%	35%	50%	75%	100%
0	1.0113	1.0339	1.0811	1.1192	–	–	–	–	–
10	1.0109	1.0330	1.0792	1.1167	1.1567	1.341	1.341	–	–
20	1.0092	1.0309	1.0764	1.1134	1.1529	1.216	1.335	1.579	1.9
30	1.0065	1.0279	1.0728	1.1094	1.1484	1.211	1.329	1.572	1.9
40	1.0029	1.0241	1.0685	1.1048	–	–	–	–	–

The Variation of the Specific Gravity of Sodium Chloride with Temperature and Concentration

%	0 °C	10 °C	25 °C	40 °C	60 °C	80 °C	100 °C
1	1.00747	1.00707	1.00409	0.99908	0.9900	0.9785	0.9651
2	1.01509	1.01442	1.01112	1.00593	0.9967	0.9852	0.9719
4	1.03038	1.02920	1.02530	1.01977	1.0103	0.9988	0.9855
8	1.06121	1.05907	1.05412	1.04798	1.0381	1.0264	1.0134
12	1.09244	1.08946	1.08365	1.07699	1.0667	1.0549	1.0420
16	1.12419	1.12506	1.11401	1.10688	1.0962	1.0842	1.0713
20	1.15663	1.15254	1.14533	1.13774	1.1268	1.1146	1.1017
24	1.18999	1.18557	1.17776	1.16971	1.1584	1.1463	1.1331
26	1.20709	1.20254	1.19443	1.18614	1.1747	1.1626	1.1492

3.13   Buffer Solution Data

Hydrochloric Acid Buffer		Acid Phthalate Buffer		Neutralized Phthalate Buffer	
To 50.0 ml of 0.2m KCL add the ml of HCL specified		To 50.0 ml of 0.2M $KCH_6H_4(COO)_2$ add the ml of HCL specified		To 50.0 ml of 0.2M $KCH_6H_4(COO)_2$ add the ml of NaOH specified	
pH	0.2M HCl, ml	pH	0.2M HCl, ml	pH	0.2M NaOH, ml
1.2	85.0	2.2	49.5	4.2	3.0
1.3	67.2	2.4	42.2	4.4	6.6
1.4	53.2	2.6	35.4	4.6	11.1
1.5	41.4	2.8	28.9	4.8	16.5
1.6	32.4	3.0	22.3	5.0	22.6
1.7	26.0	3.2	15.7	5.2	28.8
1.8	20.4	3.4	10.4	5.4	34.1
1.9	16.2	3.6	6.3	5.6	38.8
2.0	13.0	3.8	2.9	5.8	42.3
2.1	10.2	4.0	0.1	–	–
2.2	7.8	–	–	–	–

Phosphate Buffer		Alkaline Borate Buffer	
To 50.0 ml of 0.2M KH_2PO_4 add the ml of NaOH specified		To 50.0 ml of 0.2M H_3BO_3–KCl add the ml of NaOH specified	
pH	0.2M NaOH soln	pH	0.2M NaOH soln
5.8	3.6	8.0	3.9
6.0	5.6	8.2	6.0
6.2	8.1	8.4	8.6
6.4	11.6	8.6	11.8
6.6	16.4	8.8	15.8
6.8	22.4	9.0	20.8
7.0	29.1	9.2	26.4
7.2	34.7	9.4	32.1
7.4	39.1	9.6	36.9
7.6	42.4	9.8	40.6
7.8	44.5	10.0	43.7
8.0	46.1	–	–

3.14.1   Pyschrometric Chart – Normal Temperatures

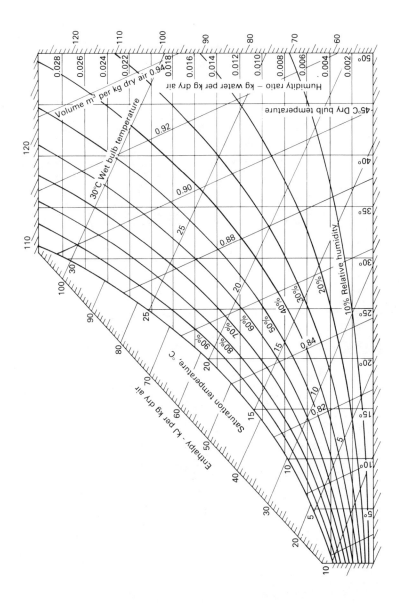

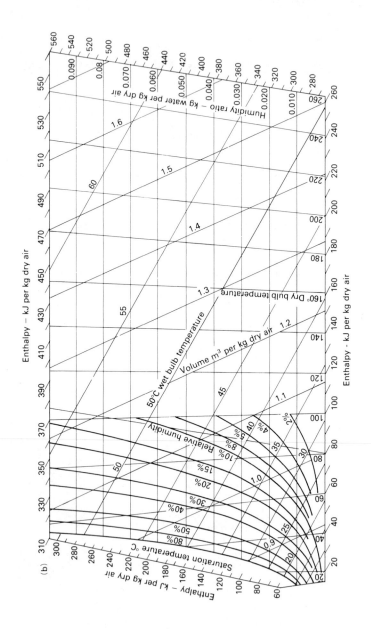

3.14.3. Depression of the Wet Bulb Tables

% Relative Humidity															Depression of the Wet Bulb °F
34	33	32	32	31	30	29	28	27	26	25	23	22	21	19	30
36	35	34	33	32	32	31	30	29	28	26	25	24	23	21	29
37	37	36	35	34	33	32	31	30	29	28	27	26	25	23	28
39	39	38	37	36	35	34	33	32	31	30	29	28	27	25	27
41	41	40	39	38	37	36	35	34	33	32	31	30	29	27	26
42	42	41	41	40	39	38	37	36	35	34	33	32	31	30	25
44	44	43	42	42	41	40	39	38	37	36	35	34	33	32	24
46	45	44	44	43	42	42	41	40	39	38	37	36	35	34	23
48	47	46	46	45	44	44	43	42	41	40	39	38	37	36	22
50	49	49	48	47	46	46	45	44	43	42	42	41	40	39	21
52	51	51	50	49	48	48	47	46	45	45	44	43	42	41	20
54	53	53	52	52	51	50	49	48	48	47	46	45	44	43	19
56	55	55	54	54	53	52	51	51	50	49	48	48	47	46	18
58	58	57	56	56	55	54	54	53	52	52	51	50	49	48	17
60	59	59	58	58	57	57	56	55	55	54	53	52	52	51	16
62	61	61	60	60	59	59	58	58	57	56	56	55	54	53	15
64	64	63	63	62	62	61	61	60	59	59	58	58	57	56	14
66	66	66	65	65	64	64	63	63	62	61	61	60	60	59	13
69	68	68	68	67	67	66	66	65	65	64	63	63	62	62	12
71	71	71	70	70	69	69	68	68	67	67	66	66	65	64	11
73	73	73	72	72	72	71	71	70	70	69	69	68	68	67	10
76	76	75	74	74	74	74	73	73	73	72	72	71	71	70	9
78	78	78	77	77	77	76	76	76	75	75	75	74	74	73	8
81	81	80	80	80	79	79	79	79	78	78	78	77	77	76	7
83	83	83	82	82	82	82	82	81	81	81	81	80	80	80	6
86	86	85	85	85	85	85	85	84	84	84	84	83	83	83	5
89	88	88	88	88	88	88	88	87	87	87	87	87	86	86	4
91	91	91	91	91	91	91	91	90	90	90	90	90	90	89	3
94	94	94	94	94	94	94	94	94	93	93	93	93	93	93	2
97	97	97	97	97	97	97	97	97	97	97	97	97	96	96	1
130	128	126	124	122	120	118	116	114	112	110	108	106	104	102	

Dry Bulb Temperature °F

continued over

% Relative Humidity																			Depression of the Wet Bulb °F
18	16	15	13	11	9	7	5	2											30
20	18	17	15	13	11	9	7	5	2										29
22	20	19	17	15	14	12	9	7	5	2									28
24	23	21	19	18	16	14	12	10	7	5	2								27
26	25	23	22	20	18	16	14	12	10	8	5	2							26
28	27	26	24	22	21	19	17	15	13	10	8	5	3						25
31	29	28	26	25	23	21	20	18	16	13	11	8	6	3					24
33	32	30	29	27	26	24	22	20	18	16	14	11	9	6	3	1			23
35	34	33	31	30	28	27	25	23	21	19	17	15	12	9	6	3			22
37	36	35	34	32	31	29	28	26	24	22	20	18	15	13	10	7	4		21
40	39	38	36	35	34	32	30	29	27	25	23	21	19	16	14	11	8		20
42	41	40	39	38	36	35	33	32	30	28	26	24	22	20	17	14	12	9	19
45	44	43	42	40	39	38	36	35	33	31	30	28	25	23	21	18	16	13	18
47	46	45	44	43	42	41	39	38	36	35	33	31	29	27	25	22	20	17	17
50	49	48	47	46	45	44	42	41	39	38	36	34	33	31	28	26	24	21	16
53	52	51	50	49	48	47	45	44	43	41	40	38	36	34	32	30	28	25	15
55	54	54	53	52	51	50	48	47	46	45	43	42	40	38	36	34	32	30	14
58	57	57	56	55	54	53	52	51	49	48	47	45	44	42	40	38	36	34	13
61	60	59	59	58	57	56	55	54	53	52	50	49	48	46	44	43	41	39	12
64	63	62	62	61	60	59	58	57	56	55	54	53	51	50	49	47	45	43	11
67	66	66	65	64	63	63	62	61	60	59	58	57	55	54	53	51	50	48	10
70	69	69	68	67	67	66	66	64	64	63	62	61	60	58	57	56	54	53	9
73	72	72	71	71	70	69	69	68	67	66	66	65	64	63	62	60	59	58	8
76	76	75	75	74	74	73	72	72	71	70	70	69	68	67	66	65	64	63	7
79	79	78	78	78	77	77	76	76	75	74	74	73	72	71	71	70	69	68	6
83	82	82	81	81	81	80	80	79	79	78	78	77	77	76	75	75	74	73	5
86	86	85	85	85	84	84	84	83	83	83	82	82	81	81	80	79	79	78	4
89	89	89	89	88	88	88	88	87	87	87	86	86	86	85	85	84	84	83	3
93	93	93	92	92	92	92	92	91	91	91	91	90	90	90	90	89	89		2
96	96	96	96	96	96	96	96	96	96	96	95	95	95	95	95	95	95	94	1
100	98	96	94	92	90	88	86	84	82	80	78	76	74	72	70	68	66	64	

Dry Bulb Temperature °F

Dry Bulb Temperature °F →	62	60	58	56	54	52	50	48	46	44	42	40	38	36	34	Depression of the Wet Bulb °F
																30
																29
																28
																27
																26
																25
																24
																23
																22
																21
																20
	5	2														19
	9	6														18
	14	11	7	3												17
	18	15	12	8	5											16
	23	20	17	13	10	6	2									15
	27	25	22	19	15	12	8	4								14
	32	29	27	24	21	17	14	10	6							13
	37	34	32	29	26	23	20	16	12	8						12
	41	39	37	35	32	29	26	23	19	15						11
	46	44	42	40	38	35	32	29	26	22	18					10
	51	49	48	46	43	41	38	36	33	30	26					9
	56	55	53	51	49	47	45	42	40	37	34	30				8
	61	60	59	57	55	53	51	49	47	44	42	39				7
	67	65	64	63	61	60	58	56	54	52	50	47	44			6
	72	71	70	69	68	66	65	63	62	60	58	56	53			5
	77	77	76	75	74	73	72	70	69	68	66	64	62	60		4
	83	82	82	81	80	79	79	78	77	75	74	73	72	70		3
	88	88	88	87	87	86	86	85	84	84	83	82	81	80	79	2
	94	94	94	94	93	93	93	92	92	92	91	91	90	90	89	1

Dry Bulb Temperature °F

3.14.4   Water Activity Table

a_w Range	Organisms inhibited by lower value	Examples of Foods having this lower a_w value
1.00-0.95	Gram-negative rods; Spores of Bacillaceae	Foods containing c.40 wt% sucrose or c.7 wt% NaCl Bread crumb
0.95-0.91	Most cocci, lacto-bacilli and vegetative cells or	Foods containing c.55 wt% sucrose or c.12wt% NaCL Raw ham
0.91-0.88	Most yeasts	Foods containing c.65 wt% sucrose or 15 wt% NaCl Salami, Fishmeal with c.10% H_2O
0.88-0.80	Most moulds Staph.aureus	Flour, rice, pulses with c. 17% H_2O Fruit cake Dry sausage
0.80-0.75	Most halophilic bacteria	Foods containing c.26 wt% NaCl Jams and Fondant creams
0.75-0.65	Xerophilic moulds	Marzipan, marshmallow Fishmeal with c.5%H_2O
0.65-0.60	Osmophilic yeasts	Liquorice, gums Medium salted cod with c.12% H_2O
< 0.60	All micro-organisms	Toffees, boiled sweets Raisins

Source: Mossel D A A, Micrbial Spoilage of Proteinaceous Foods, 1970.

3.14.5 Table of Constant Humidity Solutions

Substance Dissolved and Solid Phase	Temp ^{0}C	Humidity %
Lead Nitrate.$Pb(NO_3)_2$	20	98
Dibasic sodium phosphate $Na_2HPO_4.12H_2O$	20	95
Monobasic ammonium phosphate $NH_4H_2PO_4$	20-25	93
Zinc sulphate $ZnSO_4$.$7H_2O$	20	90
Potassium chromate K_2CrO_4	20	88
Potassium bisulphate $KHSO_4$	20	86
Potassium bromide KBr	20	84
Ammonium sulphate $(NH_4)_2SO_4$	20	81
Ammonium chloride NH_4Cl	20-25	79
Sodium acetate $NaC_2H_3O_2.3H_2O$	20	76
Sodium chlorate $NaClO_3$	20	75
Sodium nitrite $NaNO_2$	20	66
Sodium bromide NaBr. $2H_2O$	20	58
Magnesium nitrite $Mg(NO_3)_2.6H_2O$	18.5	56
Potassium thiocyanate KSCN	20	47
Zinc nitrate, $Zn(NO_3)_2.6H_2O$	20	42
Chromium trioxide, CrO_3	20	35
Calcium chloride, $CaCl_2.6H_2O$	24.5	31
Potassium acetate, $KC_2H_3O_2$	20	20
Lithium chloride, $LiCl.H_2O$	20	15

Source: The Merck Index, 8th Edit (1968), Merck and Co, Rahway, NJ.

3.14.6 Classification of Common Drier Types

Drier Type	Usual Food Type
Air Convection Driers	
air lift	small pieces granules
belt trough	pieces
cabinet, tray or pan	pieces, purees, liquids
continuous conveyor belt	purees, liquids
fluidized bed	small pieces, granules
kiln	pieces
spray	liquids, purees
tunnel	pieces
Drum or Roller Driers	
atmospheric	purees, liquids
vacuum	purees, liquids

continued over

Drier Type	Usual Food Type
Vacuum Driers	
freeze driers	pieces, liquids
vacuum belt	purees, liquids
vacuum shelf	pieces, purees

Source: Potter Norman N (Editor) 1973, Food Dehydration and Concentration,   In
Food Science, 2nd Edit, Avi Publishing Co, Westport, Conn.

3.14.7   Moisture and Weight Relationship Due to Drying

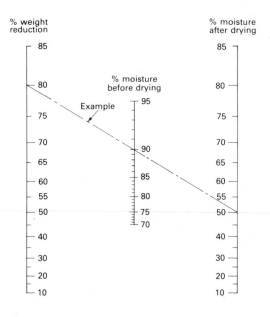

4 Food Thermal Data

4.1   Estimation of the Thermal Properties of Foods

A working group was set up recently as a sub–committee of COST 90 in order to examine the proposition that the thermal properties of a food could be estimated from a knowledge of its nature and state, such as its chemical composition, temperature and density.

The first tasks for the working group were to compile a list of published equations for predicting enthalpy, specific heat, ice content, thermal conductivity and density; to convert the equations to a common system of units; to note any comments of the authors on their applicability; and to collect data and equations for the thermal properties of food components.

In order to assess the robustness of such equations for use with foodstuffs, a limited comparison between the actual and the computed properties was carried out.   A brief description of a computer program for estimating certain properties on the basis of selected equations, is included with permission of the authors.

4.2   Formulae and Computer Program

Selected Equations

The following equations were selected on the basis of the comparison between actual and computed properties for a limited range of foodstuffs.

$T > T_f$

$$\lambda = \sum \epsilon_i \chi_i \qquad \qquad \lambda(1.20)$$

$$h = \sum c_i \chi_i T \qquad \qquad h(1.3)$$

$$c = \sum c_i \chi_i \qquad \qquad c(1.10)$$

All   T

$$\alpha = \frac{\lambda}{\rho c} \qquad \qquad \alpha(3.1)$$

$$P(c = o) = \frac{1}{\sum \dfrac{\chi_i}{P_i}} \qquad \qquad p(1.2)$$

$T < T_f$

$$\lambda = \sum \epsilon_i \chi_i$$

$$h = c_s(1 - \chi_w)(T - T_f) + c_w \chi_w T_f \ln \frac{T}{T_f}$$

$$- c_{ice}\chi_w(T - T_f) - c_{ice}\chi_w T_f \ln \frac{T}{T_f}$$

$$\left[1 - \frac{T_f}{T} \right] + T_f \sum c_i \chi_i \qquad \qquad h(2.2)$$

$$c = c_s(1 - \chi_w) + c_w \chi_w \frac{T_f}{T} + c_{ice}\left[1 - \frac{T_f}{T} \right]\chi_w - L\chi_w\frac{T_f}{T} \qquad \qquad c(2.3)$$

Bulk Products

$$\lambda(bulk) = (1 - \epsilon(bulk)) \times \lambda$$

In order to execute the computer program the following input is required.

- the composition of the food ie % water, % fat, etc
- the density (at 20°C)
- the initial freezing point

Program Format by Example

1	Cereals	8	Sugars
2	Milk, Eggs	9	Fruits
3	Fat, Oil	10	Beverages
4	Meat	11	Sauces, Soups
5	Fish	12	Confectionary
6	Vegetables	13	Cheese
7	Nuts	14	Miscellaneous

***** Which product group ? : 9

      Product name   : strawberry

Water content (%)

1	moist	70-100	2	semi-moist	40-69.9
3	semi-dry	20- 39.9	3	dry	0-19.9

*** Which group ? : 1

Composition known (0=NO; 1=Yes) : 1

Dry base (0) or Wet base (1) ? : 1
Type composition in %
If a component is not available type a negative number.

Water	:	92
Protein	:	0
Fat	:	0
Carbohydrates	:	8
Minerals	:	0

CONTROL

Component	% (input)	% Default	Real Fraction
Water	92.0		0.920
Protein	0		0.000
Carbohydrates	8.0		0.080
Minerals	0		0.000
Total wet base	100.000		

```
Is product solid (1) or liquid (2) ? : 1
Homogeneous (1) or bulk (2) ? : 2
Density of homogeneous product (kg/m **3) ?
If not available type zero  : 0
Equivalent diameter of homogeneous product (cm) : ?
If not available type zero : 4
Density of bulk (kg/m**3) : ?
If not available type zero : 0
Initial freezing point (degrees C) : ?
If not available type a positive value : -.5
Questions about the output :

Specific Temperatures (1) or Range (2) ? : 2
Type lower-, upper limit and temperature step separated by a
comma : -40, 40, 5.
Desired properties (0=NO and 1=YES) :
Conductivity    ?  : 1
Diffusivity     ?  : 1
Enthalpy        ?  : 1
Specific Heat   ?  : 1
```

End of input

Computer output

Bulk Product	:	Strawberry
Composition (fractions)	:	
Water	:	0.920
Protein	:	0.000
Fat	:	0.000
Carbohydrates	:	0.080
Minerals	:	0.000
Freezing point	:	-0.50 Degrees C

Thermal Properties of Strawberry - Computer Prediction

Temp °C	Thermal Conductivity W/m °K	Thermal Diffusivity m²/s	Enthalpy kJ/kg	Specific Heat kJ/kg °K
-40.0	1.489	0.1353E-05	-359.8	2.033
-35.0	1.450	0.1298E-05	-349.5	2.064
-30.0	1.413	0.1237E-05	-339.1	2.110
-25.0	1.375	0.1162E-05	-328.4	2.186
-20.0	1.338	0.1064E-05	-317.2	2.322
-15.0	1.299	0.9175E-06	-304.9	2.613
-10.0	1.255	0.6745E-06	-290.2	3.427
-5.0	1.183	0.2804E-06	-265.8	7.744
0.0	0.3345	0.1433E-06	0.000	3.978
5.0	0.3392	0.1451E-06	19.89	3.978
10.0	0.3439	0.1474E-06	39.78	3.978
15.0	0.3486	0.1496E-06	59.67	3.978
20.0	0.3533	0.1518E-06	79.56	3.978
25.0	0.3580	0.1540E-06	99.45	3.978
30.0	0.3628	0.1563E-06	119.3	3.978
35.0	0.3675	0.1583E-06	139.2	3.978
40.0	0.3722	0.1608E-06	159.1	3.978

Limitations of the Computer Program

The initiators of the computer program acknowledge that since much of the thermal data reported has limited information about the nature and state of the food, it was not possible to test the program adequately. Another problem encountered was the requirement in some instances to estimate the bound or unfreezable water content of the food. As a temporary solution the amount of unfreezable water was estimated using the following equation;

$$X_{(bound\ water)} = 0.3X_p + 0.1X_c$$

where X_p = mass fraction proteins, and X_c = mass fraction carbohydrates

4.3 Tabulated Values of the Thermal Properties of Foods

Most of the data in the following section has been extracted from an article published in 'Food Technology', November 1980, entitled 'A Compilation of the Thermal Properties of Foods' by S L Polley; O P Snyder, and P Kotnour.

The data on starches was collected by my industrial colleagues at CPC (United Kingdom) Ltd.

4.3.1 Thermal Properties of Fish, Meat and Poultry

Food	%H$_2$O	F P °C	Specific Heat (kJ/kg °C) Above Freezing	Specific Heat (kJ/kg °C) Below Freezing	Thermal Conductivity (W/m °K)	Latent Heat
FISH						
Cod, fresh	–	-2.2	3.770	2.050	–	277
Cod, fried	60	–	3.020	–	–	–
Cod, frozen	70	-2.2	3.180	1.720	–	235
Fillets						
Haddock	80	–	3.520	1.840	–	–
Mackerel	57	–	2.760	1.550	–	–
Ocean perch	80	–	3.520	1.840	–	–
Pollock	79	–	3.480	1.840	–	–
Whiting	82	–	3.600	1.840	–	–
Fish, dried	70	-2	3.180	1.717	–	235
Shellfish						
Lobster	79	–	3.480	1.840	–	–
Oyster	80.4	-3	3.480	1.840	–	270
Oyster, tub	87	-3	3.770	1.930	–	291
Scallop	80.3	–	3.520	1.840	–	270
Scallops	80.3	-2.2	3.730	2.010	–	270
Shrimp	70.8	-2.2	3.480	1.880	–	277
Tuna	70	–	3.180	1.720	–	–

continued over

Food	%H_2O	F P °C	Specific Heat (kJ/kg °C)		Thermal Conductivity (W/m °K)	Latent Heat
			Above Freezing	Below Freezing		

MEATS

Food	%H_2O	F P °C	Above Freezing	Below Freezing	Thermal Conductivity	Latent Heat
Bacon	57	–	2.010	–	–	–
Bacon, fresh lean	68	-1.7	3.220	1.680	–	233
Bacon, smoked	13-29	–	1.26-1.8	1.0-1.2	–	42-96
Beef						
Dried	5-15	–	0.92-1.4	0.7-1.1	–	16-52
Fresh fat	–	-2.2	2.510	1.470	–	184
Lamb						
Fresh	60-70	-2.2	2.8-3.2	1.5-2.2	0.41-0.48	194-276
Livers	65.5	-1.7	3.02	1.68	–	217
Pork						
Fresh	60-75	-2	2.85	1.6	0.44-0.54	201
Sausage						
Drying	65.5	-3.3	3.73	2.35	–	216
Franks	60	-1.7	3.73	2.35	–	200
Fresh	65	-3.3	3.4-3.7	2.35	–	–
Smoked	60	-3.9	3.60	2.35	–	200
Veal	58-80	-2	2.95-3.4	1.6-2.0	–	211

POULTRY

Food	%H_2O	F P °C	Above Freezing	Below Freezing	Thermal Conductivity	Latent Heat
Fresh and frozen	74	-2.8	3.31	1.55	–	247

4.3.2   Thermal Properties of Other Foods

NB Thermal conductivity at stated temperatures (suffix).

Food	%H_2O	F P ^oC	Specific Heat (kJ/kg ^oC) Above Freezing	Below Freezing	Thermal Conduct- ivity (W/m ^oK)	Latent Heat
Apples	84	-2	3.60	1.8-1.9	0.4153_{60}	280-282
Apricots	85.4	-2	3.68	1.93	–	284
Artichokes						
Globe	83.7	-2	–	1.88	–	279
Jerusalem	79.5	-2.5	3.48	1.84	–	265
Asparagus	93.0	-1.2	3.94	2.01	–	310-312
Avacados	94.0	-2.7	3.81	2.05	–	316
Bananas	74.8	-2.2	3.35	1.76	–	251-255
Beans, dried	12.5	–	1.35	1.01	–	42
Beans, fresh	90.0	-18	3.94	2.39	–	297
Beans, Lima	66.5	-1.1	3.06	1.68	–	219
Beans, string	88.9	-1.3	3.81	1.97	–	298
Beets	87.6	-2.8	3.77	1.68	–	293
Blackberries						
Logan	82-85	-30	3.6-3.7	1.68-1.9	–	284
Blueberries	82.3	-1	3.6	1.88	–	275
Bread, white	44-45	-2	2.72-2.93	1.42	–	109-121
Broccoli	89.9	-1.6	3.85	1.97	–	302
Brussel						
sprouts	84.9	-0.6	3.68	1.67	–	284
Cabbage	92.4	-0.5	3.94	1.97	–	306-307
Cantaloupe	92.7	-1.7	3.94	2.01	–	307
Carrots	88.2	-1.3	3.6-3.8	1.8-1.9	–	293
Cauliflower	91.7	–	3.89	1.97	–	307
Celeriac	88.3	–	3.81	1.93	–	293
Celery	93.7	-1.3	3.98	2.01	–	314
Cheese	37-38	-2.2	2.09	1.30	–	126
Limburger	55	-7.2	2.93	1.68	–	200
Roquefort	55	-16.1	2.72	1.34	–	184
Swiss	55	-9.4	2.68	1.51	–	184
Nonfat	50	–	2.68	1.47	–	–
Cherries	83	-3.3	3.65	1.89	–	279
Chocolate						
coating	55	–	1.26	2.30	–	93
Corn, dried	10.5	–	1.17	0.96	–	35
Corn, green	73.9	-1.7	3.31	1.76	–	247
Cranberries	87.4	-2.6	3.77	1.93	–	288
Cream						
Ice cream	58-66	-3-18	3.3	1.88	–	222
Sweetened	75	–	3.56	2.09	–	–
40% fat	73	-2.2	3.56	1.68	–	209

continued over

Food	%H_2O	F P °C	Specific Heat (kJ/kg °C) Above Freezing	Below Freezing	Thermal Conductivity (W/m °K)	Latent Heat
Sour cream	57–73	–	2.93	1.26	–	–
Cream cheese	80	–	2.93	1.88	–	–
Curd, cheese cottage	60–70	–	3.27	–	–	–
Dates, dried	20	–20	1.51	1.09	–	67.5
Egg, crated	–	–3	3.18	1.68	–	233
Egg	–	–3	3.2	1.67	0.33–0.97	276
Eggplant	92.7	–0.9	3.94	2.01	–	307
Endive	93.3	–0.6	3.94	2.01	–	307
Figs, dried	24	–	1.63	1.13	–	79
Figs, fresh	78	–2.7	3.43	1.80	–	261
Flour	12–13.5	–	1.8–1.9	1.17	–	–
Wheat	8.8	–	–	0.450	–	
Garlic, dry	74.2	–3.7	3.31	1.76	–	247
Gooseberry	88.3	–1.7	3.77	1.93	$0.28–0.33_{-16}$	293
Grapefruit	88.8	–2	3.81	1.93	–	293
Grapes, USA	81.9	–2.5	3.60	1.84	–	270
Horseradish	73.4	–3.1	3.27	1.76	–	247
Kohlrabi	90.1	–1.1	3.85	1.98	–	298
Leeks, green	88.2	–1.6	3.77	1.93	–	293
Lemons	89.3	–2.2	3.85	1.93	–	295
Lettuce	94.8	–0.4	4.02	2.01	–	316
Limes	86	–1.7	3.73	1.93	–	284
Macaroni	12–14	–	1.84	1.88	0.490	–
Mangoes	93	0	3.77	1.93	–	312
Maple sugar	5	–	1.01	0.88	–	16.3
Maple syrup	36	–	2.05	1.30	–	121
Margarine	9–15	–	1.8–2.1	–	0.234	–
Melon	92.6	–6.7	3.94	2.01	–	307
Muskmelon	92.7	–1.7	3.94	2.01	–	307
Watermelon	92.1	–1.6	4.06	2.01	–	307
Milk	87.5	–0.6	3.89	2.05	–	288
Mushrooms	91.1	–1	3.89	1.97	–	302
Nectarines	82.9	–1.7	3.77	2.05	0.585_9	277
Nuts, dried	3–10	–	0.8–1.2	0.8–1.0	–	10–32
Olives	75.2	–1.9	3.35	1.76	–	251
Onions	87.5	–1.1	3.77	1.93	–	288
Oranges	87.2	–2.2	3.77	1.93	$0.415_{15.6}$	288
Orange juice	89	–1.2	3.89	–	$0.544_{15.6}$	–
Parsnips	78.6	–1.7	3.52	1.93	–	261
Peaches	86.9	–1.4	3.77	1.93	–	288
Pears	83.5	–1.9	3.60	1.88	–	275
Peas, dried	9–14	–	1.1–1.8	0.9–1.9	–	33
Peas, green	74.3	–1.1	3.31	1.76	$0.502_{15.6}$	247

Food	%H_2O	F P °C	Specific Heat (kJ/kg °C)		Thermal Conductivity (W/m °K)	Latent Heat
			Above Freezing	Below Freezing		
Peppers	92.4	-1.1	3.94	1.97	–	307
Persimmons	78.2	-2.1	3.52	1.80	–	261
Pineapples	85.3	-1.4	3.68	1.88	0.5486	284
Plums	85.7	-2.2	3.68	1.88	0.24-0.55	286
Pomegranate	77	-2.2	3.68	2.01	–	261
Potatoes	77.8	-1.7	3.43	1.80	0.42-1.1	258
Pumpkins	90.5	–	3.85	1.97	–	302
Quinces	85.3	-2.2	3.68	1.88	–	284
Radishes	93.6	–	3.98	2.01	–	312
Rasberries	82	-1.1	3.56	1.88	–	284
Rhubarb	94.9	-2	4.02	2.01	–	312
Rice	10-14	–	–	1.7-1.9	–	–
Salsify	79.1	-2	3.48	1.84	–	263
Spinach	85-93	-1	3.94	2.01	–	307
Starch, corn	–	–	1.2-1.3	–	$0.12-0.2_{25}$	–
Strawberry	90	-1.2	3.89	1.1-2.0	$0.67-1.2_{13,-18}$	290
Strawberry juice	92	-1	3.98	–	$0.571_{15.6}$	–
Sweet potatoes	68.5	-2	3.14	1.68	–	226
Tangerines	87.3	-2.2	3.89	2.09	–	293
Tomatoes	94	-1	3.98	2.01	0.46-0.53	312
Turnips	90.9	-1	3.89	1.97	0.56	–

4.3.3   Thermal Properties of Fresh Fruit, Vegetables and Juices

Product	Water Content %	Thermal Conduct- ivity W/m K	Apparent Density kg/m^3	Mean Specific Heat	Thermal Diffusity m^2/s x 10^7
Apples	84–85	0.415	878	3.77	1.25
Apple juice	87.2	0.554	1051	3.85	1.37
Apple juice concentrate	49.8	0.433	1227	3.01	1.17
Apple sauce	82.8	–	–	3.73	–
Bilberry juice	89.5	0.554	1041	3.89	1.37
Cherry juice	86.7	0.554	1052	3.85	1.37
Grapefruit	84.7	0.537	1062	3.81	1.33
Oranges	87.2	0.415	878	3.77	1.25
Orange juice	89.0	0.554	1043	3.89	1.37
Raspberry juice	88.5	0.554	1046	3.89	1.36
Strawberry juice	91.7	0.571	1033	3.98	1.39

Adapted from data published by Gane (1936), Riedel (1951) and Slavicek et al (1962).

Thermal diffusivity calculated from data presented.

4.3.4   Thermal Conductivity of Heating Media Used in Food Processing

Heating Medium	Temperature ^{0}C	Thermal Conductivity
Ice	-25	2.42
	0	1.28
Water (liquid)	0	0.594
	37.8	0.628
	93	0.680
Air	0	0.024
	100	0.032
	200	0.039
Olive Oil	20	0.168
	100	0.164
Sodium Chloride brine		
(25%)	30	0.571
(12.5)	30	0.588
Nitrogen	-100	0.016
	0	0.024
	100	0.031
Sulphur dioxide	0	0.023
	100	0.031
Water vapour (saturated)	0	0.023
	93	0.028
	204	0.034
	315.6	0.044

Adapted from References:

Keith, Frank: Principals of Heat Transfer, International Text Book Co, Scranton, Pa.
McAdams, William H: Heat Transmission, McGraw-Hill Book Co.
Perry, John H: 1950, Chemical Engineer's Handbook, McGraw-Hill, 3rd Edit.

4.3.5 Thermal Properties of Food Container Materials

Material	Thermal Conductivity W/m ^{0}K	Specific Heat kJ/kg ^{0}K	Apparent Density kg/m^3	Thermal Diffusivity m/s x 10^7
Aluminium	202.5-268.2	0.963	2700	537 x 10^2
Glass, (borosilicate)	1.125	0.837	2243	5.99
Nylon (type 6/6)	0.242	1.675	1121	1.29
Polyethylene (HD)	0.485	2.303	961	2.19
Polyethylene (LD)	0.329	2.303	929	1.54
Polypropylene	0.118	1.926	913	0.67
Teflon	0.260	1.217	2082	1.03
Stainless Steel type (302)	15.87	0.494	7912	40.6
Steel	36-45	0.502	7100	114
Tin	57-62	-	-	-

4.3.6 Thermal Diffusivity of Some Foodstuffs

Product	Water wt%	Temperature ^0C	Thermal Diffusivity $m^2/s \times 10^7$
Fruits and Vegetables			
Apple, whole, Red Delicious	85	0-30	1.37
Apple sauce	37	5	1.05
Apple sauce	37	65	1.12
Apple sauce	80	5	1.22
Apple sauce	80	65	1.40
Apple sauce	–	26-129	1.67
Avacado, flesh	–	24, 0	1.24
Avacado, seed	–	24, 0	1.29
Avacado, whole	–	41, 0	1.54
Banana, flesh	76	5	1.18
Banana, flesh	76	65	1.42
Beans, baked	–	4-122	1.68
Cherries, tart, flesh	–	30, 0	1.32
Potato, mashed, cooked	78	5	1.23
Strawberry, flesh	92	5	1.27
Meat and Fish Products			
Codfish	81	5	1.22
Codfish	81	65	1.42
Corned beef	65	5	1.32
Corned beef	65	65	1.18
Beef, chuck	66	40-65	1.23
Beef, round	71	40-65	1.33
Beef, tongue	68	40-65	1.47
Halibut	76	40-65	1.47
Ham, smoked	64	5	1.18
Ham, smoked	64	40-65	1.38
Water	–	30	1.48
Water	–	65	1.60

Adapted from Ashrae (1981) and Gaffney et al (1980).

4.4 Enzyme Activation and Deactivation Energies

Reaction	Catalyst	Activation Energy Cal/mole required
H_2O_2 decomposition	None	18,000
	Colloidal platinum	11,700
	Liver catalase	5,500
Casein hydrolysis	HCl	20,600
	Trypsin	12,000
Sucrose inversion	Hydrogen ions	26,000
	Yeast invertase	11,500
Ethyl butyrate hydrolysis	Hydrogen ions	13,200
	Pancreatic lipase	4,200

Enzyme	Heat Inactivation Energy cal/mole
Catalase (blood)	45,000
Amylase (malt)	42,500
Lipase (pancreatic)	46,000
Bromelin	76,000
Sucrase	100,000
Trypsin	41,000

Food	Organisms Commonly Found in Spoiled Foods
Milk and milk products	Streptococci; Lactobacilli; Microbacterium; Achromobacter; Pseudomonas and Flavobacterium; Bacilli
Fresh meat	Achromobacter; Pseudomonas and Flavobacterium; Micrococci; Cladosporium; Thamnidium
Poultry	Achromobacter; Pseudomonas and Flavobacterium; Micrococci; Penicillium
Smoked, cured meats	Micrococci; Lactobacilli; Streptococci; Debaryomyces; Penicillium
Fish, shrimp	Achromobacter; Pseudomonas and Flavobacterium; Micrococci
Shellfish	Achromobacter; Pseudomonas and Flavobacterium; Micrococci
Eggs	Pseudomonas; Cladosporium; Penicillium; Sporotrichum
Vegetables	Penicillium; Rhizopus; Lactobacilli; Achromobacter; Pseudomonas and Flavobacterium
Fruit and juices	Saccharomyces; Torulopis; Botrytis; Penicillium; Rhizopus; Acetobacter; Lactobacilli

Thermophile	Industrial Significance	Growth Temps ^0C*	
Streptococcus thermophilus	Grow during milk pasteurisation; Swiss cheese, ripening agent	48	25-60
Lactobacillus bulgaricus	Bulgaricus milk, lactic acid manufacture	49	25-60
Lactobacillus thermophilus	Grow during milk pasteurisation	55	30-65
Lactobacillus delbrukii	Acidification of brewery mash, lactic acid manufacture	45	21-60
Bacillus calidolactis	Coagulates milk at high temps	55+	45-75
Bacillus thermoacidurans	Flat sour spoilage-tomato juice	45	25-60
Bacillus stearothermophilus	Flat sour spoilage-canned foods	50	45-76
Clostridium thermosaccharolyticum	Hard swells of canned foods	55+	43-71
Clostridium nigrificans	Sulphide-stinkers of canned foods	55	26-70

First temp = optimum growth temp; Second temp = growth range.

4.6   Heat Processing Data for Some Important Spoilage Organisms

Organism	°F	(°C)	D_0 (Min)	Z°F	m	Type of product needing protection against the organism
C.botulinum	250	(121)	0.1-0.3	15-18	12	Low acid foods (pH > 4.5)
C.sporogenes	250	(121)	0.8-1.5	16-20	5	Meats
B.stearothermophillis	250	(121)	4-5	17-18	5	Vegetables, milk
C.thermosaccharolticum	250	(121)	3-4	13-19	5	Vegetables
B.subtilis	250	(121	~0.4	12	6	Milk products
B.coagulans	250	(121)	0.01-0.07	18	5	Foods of pH 4.2-4.5 (tomato)
C.pasteurianum	212	(100)	0.1-0.5	15	5	Foods of pH 4.2-4.5 eg pears

NB The figures are intended to be indicative only. Specialist literature should be consulted for more precise information on particular products.

Food Product	Calorific Value Calories/100g
CEREALS	
Bread, brown	242
Bread, white	243
Flour, Manitoba, wholemeal	339
Flour, Manitoba, white	350
Oatmeal	404
Rice, polished	361
DAIRY PRODUCTS	
Butter	793
Cheese, Cheddar	425
Cheese, Gorgonzola	393
Eggs	163
Milk, fresh, whole	66
MEATS	
Beef, corned	231
Beef, frozen, raw	151
Beef, steak, raw	177
Liver, raw	143
FRUITS	
Apples, English, eating	45
Apricots, dried	183
Bananas	77
Currants, black, raw	29
Currants, red, raw	21
Gooseberries, green, raw	17
Grapefruit	22
Oranges	35
VEGETABLES	
Beans, butter, raw	266
Beans, runner, raw	15
Cabbage, savoy, raw	26
Carrots, old, raw	23
Peas, fresh, raw	64
Potatoes, old, raw	87
NUTS	
Peanuts	603
Walnuts	549

4.8 Dielectric Properties of Foods

The basic dielectrical properties of foods are related to their chemical and physical structure and are highly temperature and frequency dependent.

Biological materials such as food commodities may be considered as non-ideal capacitors in that they possess the ability to store and dissipate electrical energy from an electrical field, through a group of electrical properties expressed by the complex and collective term 'dielectric permittivity'.

The dielectric permittivity of a material is a property expressed by means of a real component, the dielectric constant, and an imaginary component, termed the dielectric loss.

$$e^x = e^x - je_{eff}$$

Food	T°C	%H$_2$O (DB)	10^{7}Hz e'	10^{7}Hz e''	10^{9}Hz e'	10^{9}Hz e''	3 x 10^{9}Hz e'	3 x 10^{9}Hz e''
Beef steak bottom, round	25	-	50	1300	50	39	40	12
Beef steak, frozen, lean	0	-	-	-	4.4	0.72	3.95	0.3
Bacon fat, conventional, rendered	25	-	-	-	2.6	0.16	2.5	0.13
Potato, raw	25	-	80	47.8	65.1	19.6	53.7	15.7
Turkey cooked	25	-	-	-	46.0	68.0*	40.0	14.0*
Butter	0	16.5	-	-	-	-	4.05	0.39
Butter	35	-	-	-	-	-	4.15	0.44
Water ice, pure	-12	-	3.7	0.07	-	-	3.2	0.003
distilled	25	-	-	-	77.5	1.2*	76.7	12.0
Distilled water + 0.5 molal	95	-	-	-	52.0	0.364	52.0	2.44
NaCl	25	-	-	-	69.0	269.0	67.0	41.87
Milk Powder	30	3.3*	-	-	-	-	2.29	0.05*
Whey Powder	30	4.8*	-	-	-	-	2.04	0.025*

NB H$_2$O * = % on wet basis.
Table adapted from von Hippel (1954) MIT Press.

5 Food Processing, Storage and Packaging Data

5.14   Recommended Storage Conditions

5.14.1 Frozen Food Storage Data
5.14.2 Frozen Meat Storage Data
5.14.3 Modified Atmosphere Storage

5.1   Glossary of Canning Terms and Definitions

Actual overlap
The amount of overlap between the end hook and the body hook.

Base plate load
Lifter Pressure
The force of the base plate which holds the can body and end component against the chuck during the seaming operation.

Beaded can
A can which is reinforced by having regular ring indentations around the body.

Body
Principal part of a container or can – usually the largest part in one piece forming the sides.

Body hook
That portion of the can body that is turned back for the formation of the double seam.

Body hook butting
The length of the body hook relative to the length of the seam.

Canners end
Packers End.   Cover.   Lid.   The end component put on in cannery.

Canners end seam
Top seam.   Packers end seam.   The double seam of the can put on by the canner.

Chuck
Seaming chuck.   Part of a double seamer or closing machine which supports the chuck wall of the end component during seaming.

Chuck wall impression
A ridge formed on the inside of the can body and contained within the double seam.   It is an impression of the chuck formed by the pressure applied by the seaming rolls during seam formation.

Closing machine
A machine which double seams canners end components on to can bodies, and which may also incorporate canners requirements such as vacuum and steam–flow conditions.

Cocked base plate
A base plate on a double seamer which is not parallel to the seaming chuck.

Compound
A sealing material consisting of a water or solvent based emulsion, or solution of either latex or synthetic rubber placed in the curl of the can end.   It fills spaces in the double seam during seaming operations, assisting in the formation of an hermetic seal.

Countersink depth
The measurement from the top edge of the seaming panel to the bottom of the chuck wall radius.

Curl
The extreme edge of an end component which is turned inwards after the end is formed. In double seaming the curl forms the end of the double seam.

Cut-over
During certain abnormal double seaming conditions, the seaming panel becomes flattened and metal is forced over the seaming chuck forming a sharp lip at the chuck wall. In extreme cases the metal may split in a cut-over.

Double seamer
Machines which double seams makers end components on to can cylinders.

External droop
Smooth projection of double seam below bottom of normal seam at the side lap. In extreme cases the external droop may be split.

Internal droop
A downward distortion of the inside end hook at the juncture.

End component
That part of a can which is used to close one or both ends of the open cylinder or can body.

End hook
That part of double seam formed from the curl of the end component.

False seam
A seam fault where the end hook and body hook are not engaged, although they give the appearance of a properly formed seam.

Feather
Sharp edge. Slight degree of cut - over. A sharp edge that may be detected with the fingernail.

First operation (Double seaming)
The first of two operations in double seaming. In this the curl of the end component is tucked under the flange of the can body and the two are rolled together.

Flange
The flared projection around the end of a can body.

Free space
The difference between the measurured seam thickness and the sum of the five plate thicknesses making up the seam.

Juncture (Cross-over)
The part of a double seam at the lap.

Knocked—down flange
A local condition similar to a false seam, in that the end hook and body hook do not engage. This is recognised by the fact that the body hook can be seen below the end hook.

Makers end
Bottom of can manufactures end component.

Makers end seam
Bottom seam. Factory end seam. The double seam of the can put on by the can manufacturer.

Mushroomed flange
A flange which is overformed and which tends to turn back at the edge.

Necked—in can
A can which has an end diameter smaller than the main body diameter. This may be at one ore both ends of the can.

Out of square body (Cocked Body)
A can body with a step in the flange due to the lap members being misaligned.

Pin Height
The distance between the highest part of the base plate and the lowest part of the seaming chuck.

Pleats
A condition occuring when the metal from the end hook folds back over itself during the first operation and is flattened to some extent by the second operation.

Pucker
This is a condition which is midway between a wrinkle and a pleat where the end hook is locally distorted downwards without actually folding.

Roll bounce (Second operation jump over)
A double seam which is not rolled tight enough adjacent to the lap. It is caused by jumping of the second operation seaming rolls at the lap.

Seam gap
The gap between the body hook and the seaming panel.

Seam length
The maximum dimensions of a seam measured parallel to the axis of a can.

Seam thickness
The maximum dimension of a seam measured at right angles to length of seam.

Second operation (Double Seaming)
The finishing operation in double seaming. The hooks formed in the first operation are ironed tight against each other in the second operation.

Side seam
The seam along the length of a can joining two edges of a blank to form a body.

Skidder
A faulty can where the seam has not been fully rolled along part of the circumfrence. This particular term is only used when a can–rotating seamer is employed.

Slipper
A condition similar to a skidder, except that this particular term applies only when a stationary can seamer is used.

Spinner
A can having in place of a completed seam, only indentations on the curl of end component and skid marks on the can body.

Spur
Localised irregularity characterised by a sharp 'V' projection at the bottom of the double seam. Usually accompanied by a pleat or a 'V' shaped pucker in the end hook.

Tightness rating
The compressive tightness of the double seam measured by rating the extent of wrinkling, puckering and pleating present in the cover hook.

Uneven hook
A body or end hook which is excessively uneven in length.

Wrinkle
Waves occuring in the end hook, may be distinguished from shadow or ghost effect by having depth.

5.2   Can Terminology

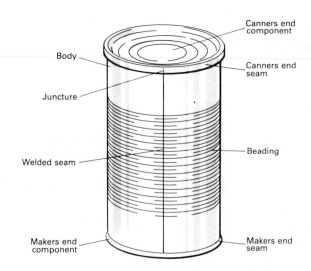

Canners end component

Body

Canners end seam

Juncture

Beading

Welded seam

Makers end component

Makers end seam

Open top processed food can

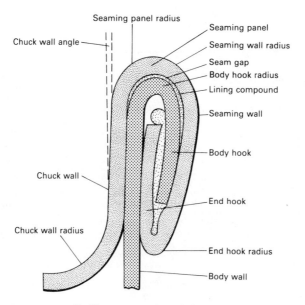

Double seam general terminology

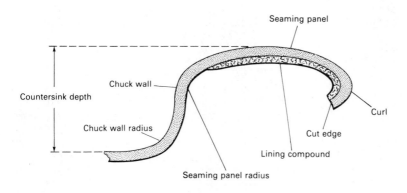

End component terminology

5.3   Can Sizes and Capacities

Can sizes are usually quoted 'Diameter x Height'. For Imperial measurements the figures used are inches and sixteenths of an inch, for example:-

401 x 411   is $4^1/_{16}$ inch diameter x $4^{11}/_{16}$ height

Metric sizes are quoted in millimetres, eg

99 x 119   is   99 mm diameter x 119 mm height

NB Capacity quoted is approximate to nearest 5 ml.   (D) =   Drawn - no lower double seam.

Imperial Size	Metric Size	Capacity (mls)
202 x 213½	52 x 72	140
211 x 202	65 x 54	155
211 x 205	65 x 54	175
211 x 301	65 x 78	235
211 x 400	65 x 102	315
211 x 414	65 x 124	385
300 x 107	73 x 37	125 (D)
300 x 108	73 x 38	125
300 x 200	73 x 51	180
300 x 201	73 x 52	185
	73 x 56.5	210 (D)
300 x 207	73 x 62	230
300 x 213	73 x 71	280
300 x 303½	73 x 82	310
300 x 312	73 x 95	355
300 x 402	73 x 105	400
300 x 405	73 x 110	425 (D)
300 x 407	73 x 113	435
300 x 408¾	73 x 115	445
300 x 604	73 x 159	630
307 x 112	83 x 44	210 (D)
307 x 200	83 x 51	235
307 x 403	83 x 106	540
307 x 408	83 x 114	580
401 x 114	99 x 48	325 (D)
401 x 200	99 x 51	325
401 x 206	99 x 60	425
401 x 210	99 x 67	445
401 x 212	99 x 70	475
401 x 400	99 x 102	720
401 x 411	99 x 119	850
401 x 509	99 x 141	1025
401 x 609	99 x 167	1215

Imperial Size	Metric Size	Capacity (mls)
401 x 614	99 x 175	1275
401 x 700	99 x 178	1295
401 x 711	99 x 195	1430
404 x 700	105 x 178	1455
502 x 711	127 x 195	2330
603 x 108	153 x 38	600 (D)
603 x 304	153 x 83	1335
603 x 402	153 x 105	1755
603 x 600	153 x 152	2630
603 x 700	153 x 178	3110
603 x 800	153 x 202	3580
603 x 904	153 x 235	4150
606 x 509	159 x 141	2570
Tapered Cans		
404 x 106	105 x 35	225 (D)
603 x 104	153 x 32	450 (D)
Oval		
-	174 x 95 x 25	240 (D)
Basin		
307 x 206	83 x 60	240 (D)
404 x 213	105 x 71	495 (D)
Tray		
-	256 x 156 x 47	1500 (D)

5.4 Recommended Food Can Sizes

Can Name	Dimensions	Products
	202 x 204	Mushrooms
	202 x 214	Babyfoods
	202 x 308	Juices (except pineapple), mushrooms, tomato paste
	202 x 314	Citrus and grape juice
	211 x 200	Olives, pimientos
	211 x 212	Mushrooms
8Z	211 x 300	Dry beans, tomato sauce
10oz	211 x 304	Fruits, juices, olives, soups, spaghetti, vegetables
	211 x 400	Dry beans, tomato sauce, meat products, (Vending) vegetables
	211 x 414	Juices, pineapple, prunes (dried)
	211 x 600	Olives
	300 x 206	Pimientos
	300 x 308	Dry beans
	300 x 400	Mushrooms
300	300 x 407	Asparagus, citrus segments, cranberries dry beans, juices (except pineapple), pimientos, spaghetti
	301 x 411	Fruits (except pineapple), vegetables,
303	303 x 406	Dry beans, fruits (except Pineapple), hominy, soups, vegetables
	303 x 509	Soups
	307 x 113	Seafoods
	307 x 203	Pineapple
	307 x 214	Dry beans
	307 x 306	Vegetables (vacuum packed), meat
	307 x 400	Dry beans, snap beans (asparagus style)
	307 x 409	Dry beans, fruits, hominy, juices, vegetables
	307 x 510	Asparagus, dry beans, mushrooms
	307 x 512	Juices (except Pineapple), soups
	307 x 704	Olives
	401 x 207.5	Pineapple
	401 x 411	Dry beans, fruits, hominy, kraut juice, olives, pimientos, soups, vegetables
303	404 x 307	Sweet potatoes, meat products
	404 x 700	All products (except pineapple)
No. 10	603 x 700	All products

5.5   Details of Tin Plate

Cans are made from steel, tinned on both sides.

Modern Electrolytical Tinplate can be produced with different tin coating weights on either side, called differential plate.   Commonly available tin coating weights:–

A	Aluminium			
N	Tin Free Steel			
	Tincoating (metric)			
Z	E.11.2.	Electrolytic		
V	E.8.4.	Electrolytic		
S	E.5,6.	Electrolytic		
L	E.4.2.	Electrolytic		
W	E.2.8.	Electrolytic		
R	E.1.4.	Electrolytic		
E	D.15.1/5.6	Diff	Electrolytic	
H	D.15.1/2.8	Diff	Electrolytic	
C	D.11.2/5.6	Diff	Electrolytic	
Q	D.11.2/3.3	Diff	Electrolytic	
G	D.11.2/2.8	Diff	Electrolytic	
D	D.8.4/5.6	Diff	Electrolytic	
5	D.8.4/3.3	Diff	Electrolytic	
M	D.8.4/2.8	Diff	Electrolytic	
T	D.5.6/11.2	Diff	Electrolytic	
J	D.5.6/2.8	Diff	Electrolytic	
P	D.2.8/5.6	Diff	Electrolytic	
1	D.2.8/3.3	Diff	Electrolytic	
3	D.1.4/2.8	Diff	Electrolytic	
K	D.2.8/5.6	Diff	Electrolytic	Reversed P
I	D.3.4/2.2	Diff	Electrolytic	Reversed

5.6   Details of Can Lacquers

The tin was originally present to assist with the can soldering construction method and to reduce the chemical interaction between the food contents and the base steel (iron) plate.   As tin levels have decreased and to minimise tin and iron dissolution into the food material, a series of internal lacquers have been developed.   These inert lacquers are selected to conform with various food requirements including:–

Non–Toxicity – usually comply to F and D A regulations.
No flavour imparted to food material.
Minimise colour changes to product.

Can lacquers are normally selected for a particular use after exhaustive testing, but it would be unwise to provide a list of actual lacquers as modern lacquer technology means that new lacquers are constantly replacing older types.   For any task consultation with a can manufacturer will provide a can with a suitable lacquer specification for the purpose intended.   Some cans are intentionally used with internally unlacquered bodies, this allows for some tin dissolution into the product which results in a 'bleaching' of the product and a 'brightening' of its colour, eg Plain internal bodies – lacquered ends: Used for tomato products, milk products, mushrooms, chicken soup, gooseberries.

Lacquer types include:

Oleoresinous   – red fruits, sulphur - resistant lacquers (formulated to have a good barrier resistance between acid products and the can metals).

Phenolic   – Meat lacquers, seafoods, (greater impermeability than oleoresinous types but minimum flexibility – unsuitable for beaded can bodies or can ends).

Epoxy   – Widely used for meats, vegatables, fruits, etc Excellent flexibility and heat stability – can be modified with phenolic for use with fruits and high fat content foods.

Epoxy-phenolic – Aluminium pigmented with meat release agent, used for cured meat products.

Organosols   – Flexible lacquers used for ends and drawn containers.

5.7   Typical Recipes and Process Details

The basis of the preservation of foods by canning continues to be the use of heat to destroy bacteria which are capable of spoiling the product, and also to destroy any pathogenic bacteria.

The pH of foods has a direct bearing on the level of heat treatment required, acid foods of pH 4.6 or below will not support the growth of food poisoning bacteria,and generally receive a heat treatment equivalent to at least 3 minutes at 250 °F (121 °C).

The development of a commercial process, (ie time/temperature combination) to produce a commercially sterile pack requires the determination of can centre temperatures under process conditions, and should be carried out by a recognised food laboratory because of the public health factors involved.   Such a heat penetration test should be completed for any change in a product formulation or can size; the rate of heat transfer may vary considerably with viscosity of product,size of particulate pieces, size of container, presence of starches, etc.   The number and type of bacteria liable to be present in the food material will also affect the heating (process) requirement, any increase in bacterial load could render a process insufficient to prevent spoilage, emphasising the need for strict principles of hygiene in food manufacture.

The details enclosed are based on experimental work carried out by the Research and Development Department of the Metal Box Company Ltd, but before any commercial production is undertaken it is recommended that the advice of a qualified canning technologist is sought.

The recipes and process details are set out using the following format:

5.7.1   Cake Canning
5.7.2   Canning Carrots
5.7.3   Notes on the Experimental Canning of Macaroni Cheese
5.7.4   Canned Minced Beef and Onions
5.7.5   Canned Rice Pudding
5.7.6   Spaghetti in Tomato Sauce
5.7.7   The Canning of Strawberries

5.7.1 Cake Canning

Method 1

a) Base and side of can lined with greaseproof paper.
b) Cake mix placed in the can which is used as a baking tin for the first part of the process.
c) The open can is placed in the oven and baked at normal oven temperature, eg 350°F to 400°F.
d) 15 minutes before the end of the normal baking time, the can is removed from the oven, a lid seamed on, and the sealed container returned to the oven to complete the full baking time.
e) After completion of the full baking period, cans are removed from the oven and allowed to air cool before final packaging.

Method 2

a), b), c), As method above.
d) 15 minutes before the end of the normal baking time, loose lids are placed in the oven to be pre-heated.
e) At the end of the full baking period, cans and loose ends are removed from the oven, the pre-heated lids seamed immediately onto the hot cans, and the sealed containers allowed to air cool before final packaging.

Both methods are intended to sterilise the can lid and reduce the possibility of mould spores surviving and developing in the finished headspace. For this reason cans must be seamed immediately, while hot, as any cooling prior to seaming could affect the vacuum and shelf-life of the product.

Obviously, in developing the product, the quantity of cake mix is calculated so that the finished risen cake does not protrude above the open can rim and therefore will not interfere with lid application.

The normal can size for cakes is 603 x 304 which contains a 900 gm finished cake.

5.7.2 Canning Carrots

Recipe and Filling Data

6.75 oz of carrots made up with brine to a total of 10.75 oz.

Brine strength − 2 oz salt; 7.5 oz sugar; made up to 5 pints with water.

Process Data

10 oz can   −   23 minutes at retort temperature of 240 °F.

16 oz can   −   30 minutes at retort temperature of 240 °F.

5.7.3 Notes on the Experimental Canning of Macaroni Cheese

Sauce	oz	gm
Cheese (dehydrated)	14	–
Full cream milk powder	6	–
Margarine	6	–
White flour	5	–
Salt	0.5	–
MSG		4
Cayenne		0.25

Water to 1 gallon

Method

Bring to the boil approximately 4.75 pints of water with margarine, salt and monosodium glutamate. Mix to a smooth paste full cream milk powder, white flour and cayenne with 1 pint of cold water. Add the mixing to batch gradually, with efficient stirring. Boil for 5 minutes. Mix the dehydrated cheese with 1 pint cold water, add to the batch carefully. Continue boiling for 2 minutes. Check bulk to 1 gallon and sieve.

Preparation of Macaroni

Boil in 1% Brine for 18 minutes. Rinse and drain, (water uptake between 180% to 200%). The cooking time and fill of macaroni may have to be adjusted according to quality and size of macaroni.

Filling and Processing Details

Fill both macaroni and sauce while hot in order to obtain a closing temperature of 170°F (minimum).

Fill per No 1 Tall can: Sauce 11 oz; Macaroni 4.5 oz

Use plain cans for this product.

Processing: 90 minutes at 240°F, then water cool.

5.7.4 Canned Minced Beef and Onions

Raw Materials	lb	oz	gm
Beef	6	8	–
White flour	–	6.5	–
Tomato puree (28% solids)	–	2	–
Salt	–	1.75	–
Protex	–	0.25	–
Caramel	–	–	10.5
Monosodium glutamate	–	–	3.5
Pepper	–	–	0.75
Thyme	–	–	0.75
Bayleaf	–	–	0.5
Sage	–	–	0.25
Water to one gallon			
Onions (reconstituted)	1	8	–

Preparation

Onions   Soak 4 oz of dehydrated sliced onion overnight, (water uptake 5:1).

Beef   Beef with approx 15% fat is minced through a 9mm plate.

Place minced beef in kettle, cover with cold water, bring slowly to boil with vigorous agitation to separate meat, boil for 5 minutes.   Add salt, tomato puree, protex, caramel and MSG.   Mix to a smooth paste the flour with 0.75 pint of cold water, add the mixing to the batch gradually with efficient stirring and boil for 5 minutes, adding salt-based spices one minute before the end of cooking.   Check bulk at 1 gallon, add onions and disperse thoroughly.

Canning Operations

Cans	Lacquered 8 oz cans.
Fill weights	7.75 oz
Filling	A minimum closing temperature of 170 °F is required.
Closing	If this is not achieved by hot filling, a short exhaust will be necessary.
Processing	Cans should be processed for 85 minutes at 240 °F. Water cool.

5.7.5 Canned Rice Pudding

Recipe and Filling Data

1.2–1.45 oz (34–41g) of rice

1.0 oz (28g) of sugar

1.0 oz (28g) water

15 oz tin, top up with milk (12.5 (350g) oz at 150°F (65°C)).

Processing

Seam on lid; shake manually or mechanically at 8–12 rpm.
Process for 30 minutes at 245°F/118°C.

5.7.6 Spaghetti in Tomato Sauce

Sauce	1b	oz
Tomato puree* (30% solids)	62	8
Sugar	21	14
Margarine	12	8
Parmesan cheese	9	6
Salt	9	6
Cornflour	7	13
Onion powder	1	9
Monosodium glutamate	–	3.5
White pepper	–	2.75
Mixed spice – 4 parts ground cinnamon	–	2.75
2 parts ground mace		
1 part ground clove		

Water to 50 gallons

Method

Bring to boil approximately 35 gallons of water, add tomato puree, sugar, salt, margarine and monosodium glutamate. Simmer for 5 minutes. Mix to a smooth paste cornflower, white pepper and mixed spice with approximately 7 gallons of cold water. Add the mixing to the gradually with efficient stiring. Boil for 5 minutes, add Parmesan cheese, disperse thoroughly, simmer for 3 minutes. Check bulk at 50 gallons. Sieve.

Spaghetti Preparation

Boil for 18 minutes in water with 1% salt added. Rinse in hot water drain thoroughly and fill can.

NB Boiling time and fill may have to be adjusted according to type of spaghetti used.

The best spaghetti and the most suited for canning is made from hard wheats which are high in gluten and ash content. This higher gluten content gives to the spaghetti the desired flavour and texture.

Filling

Per No 1 tall can: Spaghetti 5.5 oz; Sauce 10.5 oz

Per 8 oz can: Spaghetti 2.75 oz; Sauce 5.25 oz

NB To obtain a pack of good appearance and flavour the tomato puree must be of the best quality–bright colour and free from bitterness or harshness.

Filling Data

Weigh the blanched spaghetti into the cans and fill with the hot sauce. A closing temperature of $170\,^{0}F$ (minimum) is required, and this may necessitate a short exhaust.

Cans: plain cans for this product.

Processing: No 1 Tall cans – 85 minutes at $240\,^{0}F$. 8 oz (300 x 208)cans – 70 minutes at $240\,^{0}F$.

Whilst this process is adequate with respect to pathogenic organisms, it is borderline with respect to spoilage. Therefore, exemplory hygiene in preparation and canning is required and in any event the thermophilic hazard means that export would be very dangerous.

5.7.7   The Canning of Strawberries

Varieties

The best English varieties for canning are 'Sir John Paxton, Royal Sovereign, Huxley, Obserschleisen and Sterling Castle'.   Frozen strawberries may be used although the quality of the pack will be poor.

Preparation

The fruit, which should be received as fresh as possible, should be canned without delay, and it is desirable that the fruit be delivered in small chips or trays.

Whilst it is sometimes necessary to wash the fruit, this operation makes it very difficult to handle without resultant damage and it is, therefore, desirable that only fruit in first class condition is accepted at the factory.

The fruit should be plugged and freed from blemishes, and small berries should be removed.

Some canners prefer to give the fruit a light spray washing before filling into cans and this is useful as it removes any loose flesh or grit, but if done, the fruit must be well drained before filling, or the filled cans must be inverted to drain away excess water.

Filling

Canners Code of Practise suggests that the following should be the minimum weights of fruit per can:-

5 oz	-	3 oz
Picnic or 8 oz	-	4.5 oz
A 1	-	6.25 oz
E 1	-	8 oz
No 1 T	-	9.25 oz
A 2	-	11.5 oz
A 2.5	-	16.75 oz
A 10	-	64 oz
Other sizes	-	57%.

Syruping

Canners Code of Practice (as above) states that the following label designation should be used:-

	Not less than	Sugar/gallon	Sugar/gallon
Light syrup	15° Brix	1 lb 12 oz	1 lb 9 oz
Syrup	30° Brix	4 lb 5 oz	3 lb 6 oz
Heavy syrup	40° Brix	6 lb 11 oz	4 lb 3 oz
Extra heavy Syrup	50° Brix	10 lb 0 oz	6 lb 3 oz

Syrup should be added at 180°F

Colouring

Edicol Ponceau 4RS should be added at the rate of 3½ oz per 50 gallons of syrup.

Exhausting

The clinched cans should be exhausted for 6–8 minutes at 180°F, and seamed.

Processing

The seamed cans should be processed at 212°F as follows:-

	Stationary Cooker	Automatic Cooker
E 1	6–7 minutes	5–6 minutes
A 2	8–9 minutes	6–7 minutes

Cooling

The cans should be well cooled in water.

Cans

Fruit lacquered cans should be used.

5.8   Process Calculations.   Definition of Terms and Symbols

Term	Symbol	Definition
Retort temperature	RT	Bulk temperature of the process.
Initial temperature	IT	The centre temperature of the specific can for which the time/temperature data is plotted.
Process time	B_B	The time in minutes from the beginning of the process to the end of the heating period.
Heat penetration curve slope, or heating curve	f_h	The number of minutes required for the straight line portion of the heating curve plotted on semi-logarithmic paper to pass through one log cycle, ie the points (RT–n) and (RT–10n) where n can have any convenient value.
Sterilising value	F_0	The equivalent value of the process in terms of minutes at $250\,^0F$ when no time is involved in heating to $250\,^0F$, or cooling sublethal temperatures.
	(f_h/U)	Factor related to g value.
	F_i	Factor related to RT.
	g_{bh}	The number of degrees below retort temperature at which the heating curve exhibits a change of slope.
	x_{bh}	Number of minutes from the corrected beginning of the process to the point of break in the heating curve.
	g_{h2}	The number of degrees below retort temperature on a broken heating curve at the end of the heating period.

continued over

Term	Symbol	Definition
Second slope of heating curve	f_2	When the heating curve is expressed as a broken curve (two straight lines of different slope) this term represents the number of minutes required for the second portion of the curve to pass through the points (RT-n) and (RT-10n) where n can have any convenient value.
	f_h/U_{bh}	Factor related to g_{bh} value.
	r_{bh}	Factor related to g_{bh}.
	f_h/U_{bh}	Factor related to g_{h2} value.
Cooling water temperature	CW	The temperature of the cooling water (^{0}F).
Cooling curve slope	f_c	The number of minutes required for the cooling curve, when plotted on semi-log paper, to pass through the points (CW +n) and (CW+10n), where n can have any convenient value.
	U or U_0	Sterilising value in terms of minutes at retort temperature.
	U_3	Difference in sterilising value between that which obtains when heat penetration curve has a slope of f_h and when it has slope of f_2 for a g value equal to g_{bh} without considering the lethal value under the cooling portion of the curve.
	U_4	Sterilising value if heat penetration curve has single slope equal to f_2.
	g	The number of degrees below retort temperature on a simple heating curve at the end of the heating period.
	m	CW-product temperature (critical point temperature) at end of process.
	m+g	RT-CW

5.9   Commercial Sterilising Values

Product	Can Size	Sterilising Value F_0 (approx)
Cream Style corn	No 10	2-3
Mackerel in brine	301 x 401	2.9-3.6
Asparagus	A11	2-4
Tomato soup, (except cream of)	A11	3
Carrots	A11	3-4
Celery	A2	3-4
Cream	4-6-oz	3-4
Frankfurters in brine	up to 16Z	3-4
'Sterile ham'	1 and 2 lb	3-4
Babyfoods	babyfood	3-5
Beans in tomato sauce	A11	4-5
Cream soups	A1-16Z	4-5
	up to A10	6-10
Sausages in fat	up to 1 lb	4-6
Milk pudding	up to 16Z	4-10
Evaporated milk	up to 16 oz	5
Sausages, Vienna, in brine	various	5
Cream style corn	No 2	5-6
Chilli con carne	various	6
Dogfood	No 10	6
Green beans, brine packed	No 10	6
Meat loaf	No 2	6
Peas in brine	up to A2	6
Chicken, boned	A11	6-8
Herrings in tomato	ovals	6-8
Mushrooms in butter	up to A1	6-8
Peas in brine	A2-A10	6-8
Chicken fillets, in jelly	up to 16 oz	6-10
Mushrooms in brine	A1	8-10
Curried meats and vegetables	up to 16Z	8-12
Corn, whole kernel, brine packed	No 2	9
Meat pies	tapered, flat	10
Meat soups	up to 16Z	10
Sliced meat in gravy•	ovals	10
Dogfood	No 10	12
Meats in gravy	A11	12-15
Petfoods	up to 16Z	15-18
Poultry, game, whole, in brine	A2½ - A10	15-18

5.10 Trouble Shooting Chart (kindly provided by Metal Box plc, Worcester)

CAUSES	1st. Op seam too tight	1st. Op seam too loose	Seam length too long	Seam length too short	Cover hook too long	Cover hook too short	Body hook too long	Body hook too short	Countersink too deep	Countersink too shallow	Droop	Veeing	Wrinkle	Reverse wrinkle	Chuck impression too heavy	Chuck impression too light	Skidders	Cut over	Split cut over	False seam	Cover curl damaged	Knocked down flange	Mis-assembly of can and cover	Body buckling	Mushroom flange	Jumped seams	Free space too high
1st. Op.Roll — Too tight	•			•	•		•		•		•	•	•		•	•	•								•		
Too loose		•	•		•	•				•	•	•															
Profile too narrow	•			•	•		•				•				•		•								•		
Profile too wide			•	•		•			•				•	•													
Worn			•	•		•					•				•		•								•		
Bearing worn						•		•	•		•																
High relative to chuck						•					•						•								•		
Low relative to chuck									•	•							•										
2nd Op.Roll — Too tight			•			•			•			•			•	•	•								•		
Too loose				•		•		•			•			•		•									•		•
Profile too narrow				•									•														
Profile too wide			•													•											
Worn			•						•				•														
High relative to chuck									•								•										
Low relative to chuck									•								•								•		
Cam spring too weak																											•
1st/2nd Op.Roll — Arms worn/bushes worn					•																						
Bearing sluggish																	•										
In too long/not returning																	•				•	•	•	•			
Lip touching can body																	•								•		
Chuck — Dia. too great									•								•										
Radius incorrect																	•										
Flange too deep									•								•										
Dia. down or worn					•												•										
Top lip worn													•					•									
Greasy																	•										
Seaming spindle – excess vertical play									•								•	•									
Knock-off rod cam setting																						•	•				
Pin height incorrect									•	•	•						•							•		•	
Lifter — Force too weak			•		•				•								•										
Force too strong				•	•												•								•		
Spring damaged			•		•												•										
Bearings sluggish																	•								•		
Greasy																	•										
Filler lifter pressure top strong																								•			
Magazine timing																					•						
Cover feed pushers																					•		•				
Cover guide adjustment																					•	•	•				
Cover badly positioned on can																				•	•		•				
Cover guide/can guide allignment																					•		•				
Infeed chain/can feed turret timing																						•	•				
Can feed turret/seaming head timing																					•		•	•			
Machine speed too high																										•	
Poor can manufacture																								•			•
*Excessive lap solder									•									•	•								•
*Poor notch									•										•								
Underflanged bodies								•																			
Mushroom flanges					•	•									•												
Knockdown flanges									•													•					
Pre-wrinkle in cover seaming panel											•	•	•														
Cover — Poor curl									•		•		•														
Damaged curl																		•		•	•						
Cut edge too great				•			•	•																			
Cut edge too small					•	•																					
Lining compound excessive									•																		
Lining compound uneven									•																		
Body Hook — Too short				•					•						•												
Too long					•			•																			
Too long in makers end							•																		•		
Deep countersink				•																							
Product in seam											•	•			•	•	•										
Delivery/packaging poor																					•	•	•		•		
Can handling/conveyors poor																						•		•			
Incorrect greasing															•												

*Obsolete faults – side seams now welded

Temperature-Lethal Rate/minute for Z = 10 °C

°C	Lethal Rate	°C	Lethal Rate	°C	Lethal Rate
95	0.002	108.5	0.055	122.	1.226
95.5	0.003	109	0.061	122.5	1.376
96	0.003	109.5	0.069	123	1.544
96.5	0.003	110	0.077	123.5	1.733
97	0.004	110.5	0.086	124	1.944
97.5	0.004	111	0.097	124.5	2.181
98	0.005	111.5	0.109	125	2.447
98.5	0.006	112	0.122	125.5	2.748
99	0.006	112.5	0.137	126	3.081
99.5	0.007	113	0.154	126.5	3.457
100	0.008	113.5	0.173	127	3.880
100.5	0.009	114	0.194	127.5	4.353
101	0.009	114.5	0.218	128	4.885
101.5	0.011	115	0.244	128.5	5.482
102	0.012	115.5	0.274	129	6.150
102.5	0.013	116	0.308	129.5	6.901
103	0.015	116.5	0.345	130	7.745
103.5	0.017	117	0.388	130.5	8.688
104	0.019	117.5	0.435	131	9.746
104.5	0.021	118	0.488	131.5	10.940
105	0.024	118.5	0.548	132	12.269
105.5	0.027	119	0.615	132.5	13.774
106	0.030	119.5	0.690	133	15.455
106.5	0.035	120	0.774	133.5	17.331
107	0.038	120.5	0.868	134	19.455
107.5	0.043	121	0.974	134.5	21.834
108	0.049	121.5	1.093	135	24.509

continued over

Lethal Rates (^{0}F) For $Z = 18^0$C

^{0}F	Lethal Rate	^{0}F	Lethal Rate	^{0}F	Lethal Rate
200	0.002	233.5	0.121	246	0.600
201	0.002	234	0.129	246.25	0.619
202	0.002	234.5	0.138	246.5	0.639
203	0.003	235	0.147	246.75	0.660
204	0.003	235.5	0.156	247	0.681
205	0.003	236	0.167	247.25	0.703
206	0.004	236.5	0.178	247.5	0.726
207	0.004	237	0.190	247.75	0.749
208	0.005	237.5	0.202	248	0.774
209	0.005	238	0.215	248.25	0.799
210	0.006	238.5	0.230	248.5	0.825
211	0.007	239	0.246	248.75	0.854
212	0.008	239.5	0.261	249	0.880
213	0.009	240	0.278	249.25	0.909
214	0.010	240.25	0.287	249.5	0.938
215	0.011	240.5	0.297	249.75	0.969
216	0.013	240.75	0.306	250	1.000
217	0.015	241	0.316	250.5	1.07
218	0.017	241.25	0.327	251	1.14
219	0.019	241.5	0.337	251.5	1.21
220	0.022	241.75	0.348	252	1.3
221	0.024	242	0.359	252.5	1.38
222	0.028	242.25	0.371	253	1.47
223	0.032	242.5	0.384	253.5	1.56
224	0.036	242.75	0.398	254	1.67
225	0.041	243	0.408	254.5	1.78
226	0.046	243.25	0.421	255	1.9
227	0.052	243.5	0.435	255.5	2.02
228	0.060	243.75	0.450	256	2.16
229	0.068	244	0.464	256.5	2.3
230	0.077	244.25	0.479	257	2.45
230.5	0.083	244.5	0.495	257.5	2.61
231	0.088	244.75	0.511	258	2.79
231.5	0.094	245	0.527	258.5	2.97
232	0.100	245.25	0.545	259	3.16
232.5	0.107	245.5	0.562	259.5	3.37
233	0.114	245.75	0.581	260	3.6

5.12   Properties of Flexible Packaging Materials

One of the most important properties of flexible packaging materials used in the food industry is their ability to reist the passage of gases and vapours.   This permeability is reported in a range of units of which the most common are:

cc of gas at NTP through a membrane of test material, 1 square centimetre in area and 1 millimetre thick, in 1 second, under a differential pressure equivalent to 1 centimetre of mercury.

ie $cm^3/cm^2/mm/sec/cm$ Hg

Various other units are used around the above; for instance the area of test material may be quoted in Imperial units, the time scale may be different or the pressure differential may be quoted in atmospheres.

For water vapour permeability the units most often reported are :

gm/m^2/day at 25^{0}C and 75% RH

Permeation through homogeneous films of polymeric material is markedly dependent upon temperature. However, for whatever film material is involved, oxygen permeates about four times as fast as nitrogen, and carbon dioxide about twenty five times as fast. Thus one may express the permeability characteristics of any system as the product of three factors; one determined by the nature of the film, another by the nature of the gas involved and the third taking into account any interaction between the gas and the film.

Most flexible packaging materials are creased to some extent in use in high speed production processes, and these creases often reduce the barrier properties of the material (by mechanical breakdown).

Data is included overleaf relating to a range of food packaging materials.

Permeability Characteristics of Food Packages

Film Material	Permeability ($P \times 10^{10}$ cc/cm^2/mm/sec/cm/Hg)			
	N_2 at 30°C	O_2 at 30°C	CO_2 at 30°C	H_2O at 25°C at 90%
Polyvinylidene chloride (Saran)	0.0094	0.053	0.29	14.0
Polychloro-trifluoroethylene	0.03	0.10	0.72	2.9
Polyester (Mylar A)	0.05	0.22	1.53	1300
Rubber hydrochloride (Pliofilm ND)	0.08	0.30	1.7	240
Polyamide (Nylon 6)	0.10	0.38	1.6	7000
PVC (unplasticised)	0.40	1.20	10	1560
Cellulose acetate (P912)	2.8	7.8	68	75000
Polyethylene (ρ=0.954-.960)	2.7	10.6	35	130
(ρ=0.922)	19	55	352	800
Polystyrene	2.9	11	88	12000
Polypropylene (ρ=0.910)	–	23	92	680
Ethylcellulose (plasticised)	84	265	2000	130000

Heat-Seal Temperatures and Water Vapour Transmission Rates at 25/75

Material	Yield (in^2/lb)	Heat-Seal Temp °C	WVTR at 25/75 (g/m^2/day)
Papers			
Bleached Kraft (0.001 in PE coated)	7000	120	6
24/30 lb wet waxed sulphite	9500	60	40
Cellulosics			
PT 300	22000	–	400–500
MSAT 300	20000	135	4
Cellulose acetate (0.001 in)	21000	170	200
PVC			
100 low plasticised	17000	180	9
100 oriented-low plasticised	21000	shrinks at 90	16
Polyethylene			
Low density (100 gauge)	29000	120	3
High density (100 gauge)	29000	140	2
Polypropylene			
Extruded 100 gauge	31000	170	4
Oriented 75 gauge	41000	shrinks at 150	2

The Effect of Creasing on the Water—Vapour Transmission Rate of Various Packaging Materials

Material	WVTR (30°C and 90% RH)	
	Uncreased	Creased
$50g/m^3$ sulphate paper coated with $20g/m^3$ paraffin wax	3.0–5.0	120–180
$40g/m^3$ glassine coated with 12 g/m^3 paraffin wax	1.6–3.2	40–60
2 sheets of 32 g/m^3 glassine laminated /$12g/m^3$ paraffin wax	3.0–5.0	5.0–8.0
$40g/m^3$ sulphate paper extrusion coated /1 mil low density polyethylene	20–25	22–26
Coated cellulose film (400s), coated (extrusion)/2 mil LD Polyethylene	6–8	6–8
Aluminium foil extrusion coated:		
1 mil LD Polyethylene	0.5	0.8
1 mil LD Polyethylene film	18	18
1 mil MD Polyethylene film	11	12
1 mil HD Polyethylene film	6	8
Coated cellulose film, (300s)	10–13	25–40
Vinylidene chloride coated cellulose film, (300s)	8–10	8–12

NB   LD,MD,HD refer to low, medium and high density respectively.

5.13   Food Additive Data

The techniques for the manufacture and production of foods in the western world have changed dramatically within the past three ore four decades, so that in order that the products may reach the consumer in a palatable and wholesome condition it has become necessary to add other substances to the foods. These food additives have tended to become increasingly controversial over the past few years. The following section attempts to provide brief but concise details of the food additives used both in Europe and North America.

5.13.1 Glossary of Food Additive Terms

Food additives can be conveniently classified as follows;

1. Food colours
2. Food acidulants
3. Food flavours and sweeteners
4. Flour improvers, anti–staling agents and bleaches
5. Fat extenders, emulsifiers, gelling agents, stabilisers, and thickeners
6. Anti–oxidants, anti–caking agents, anti–foaming agents, sequestering and chelating agents.
7. Preservatives and anti–biotics
8. Nutritional supplements, vitamins and minerals
9. Adventitious additives

Food colours
The successful marketing of food products relies to a great extent upon the colour and appearance of the food. Thus colouring agents are often added in order to enhance the product image. However, many of these food colours are derived from coal tar and are termed "azo dyes", eg E102 Tartrazine.

Food acidulants
Acids are added to foods for a variety of reasons, eg to impart a sharp taste to the product or to adjust the pH. These acid materials may be of organic origin, (citric acid E330) or they may be inorganic deivatives, (phosphoric acid E338).

Food flavours and sweeteners
In this group are flavouring agents such as Maltol (E636), which is a naturally occurring flavouring added to bread and cakes, as well as flavour enhancers like monosodium glutamate. Many substances are added to food in order to impart a sweet taste, including glucose, fructose, and lactose and these are not regarded as permitted sweeteners. Only two of the permitted sweeteners have E numbers, (sorbitol E420 and mannitol E421).

Flour improvers, anti–staling and bleaching agents
Chemicals are added to the flour blend in order to produce an open–structed loaf of bread from a mixture of different types of wheat. Similarly substances may be added to a flour blend in order to whiten the product bread loaf, (E925 chlorine dioxide).

Fat extenders, emulsifiers and stabilisers

E322-494. In many foods the product quality may depend to a certain extent upon the level of fat incorporated, it is therefore prudent to extend or make the proportion of fat go further by adding a compound such as GMS-glyceryl monostearate. Emulsifiers are used to hold together unlike particles such as oil and water and so form a stable emulsion, eg mayonnaisse. Emulsifying agents may be derived from natural sources, eg lecithin or from synthetic sources, eg ethylene oxide condensates, (polyoxyethylene (8) stearate E430).

Anti-oxidants

Fats and oils are susceptible to oxidation, particularly those of animal origin, resulting eventually to the breakdown of the triglyceride molecule. The addition of anti-oxidants at low levels helps to delay this breakdown process, (E300-321).

Anti-caking agents

These are chemical substances added to particulate food solids such as sugar, flour and salt in order to improve their flow properties.

Anti-foaming agents

These may be added to refined oils and fats or other food liquids in order to minimise foaming and frothing at elevated temperatures. E990 (dimethyl polysiloxane) is normally added to the refined oil blend at very low levels.

Sequestering agents

Since oxidation reactions concerning foods are invariably catalysed by the presence of trace metals such as copper and iron, these metals may be rendered inactive by their sequestration with chemical compounds such as sodium gluconate, (E576).

Chelating agents

These are used to retain a trace metal in solution and prevent precipitation, (E385).

Preservatives and anti-biotics

E200-290. A wide range of chemical compounds may be added to foods in order to inhibit the growth of micro-organisms. Anti-biotics are compounds that inhibit growth of bacteria but are usually produced by other organisms.

Nutritional supplements, vitamins and minerals

These include vitamin concentrates of C,E, the B vitamins etc.

Adventitious additives

These include those substances added to food by default or plant malfunction.

5.13.2 Additives Permitted in the United States

The following is a partial list of chemical food additives generally recognised as safe (GRAS) by the Food and Drug administration when used according to accepted cooking procedures or as used in good commercial practice.

Acacia gum
Acetic acid (dilute)
Agar-Agar
Aluminum and potassium sulphate (alum)
Aluminum sodium sulphate
Amino acids which are normal constituents in foods
Baking powder
Baking soda
Bay leaves
Brandy
Butter
Calcium carbonate
Calcium sulphate
Caramel
Carbon dioxide
Carragheen
Citric acid
Cloves
Coffee
Corn oil
Corn starch
Corn syrup
Cottenseed oil

Cream
Cream of tartar
Dextrin
Dicalcium orthophosphate
Dried skim milk
Ethyl vanillin
Gelatin
Glycerin
Karaya gum
Lard
Lecithin
Lemon juice
Lemon extract
Mace
Magnesium carbonate
Margarine
Methyl-and propyl-para-hydroxy-benzoates
Molasses
Monocalcium phosphate
Mono- and di-glycerides of the fat-forming fatty acids (except lauric)
Mustard
Nitrogen gas
Oat gum

These chemicals would have to be used so that the food complies with all sections of the Federal Food Drug and cosmetic act. It is understood that each substance should be of food grade.

The following is a partial list of chemicals that have been accepted for the use in foods by the Food and Drug administration, or for the use in meats by the Meats Inspection Division, provided their use does not deceive or render the food adulterated or mis branded under sections of the act other than Sec. 402 (a) (2).

Antifoam A	Not more than 10ppm.
Benzoic acid	0.1%
Benzoate of soda	0.1%
Butylated hydroxyanisole[2]	In meat products, not over 0.01% of the fat content of the meat; in other food, not over 0.02% of the fat content of the food.
Butylated hydroxytoluene[2]	Not over 0.01% of the fat content of the food.
Calcium propionate or sodium propionate or any mixture of the two	In bread, not more than 0.32 part for each 100 parts by weight of flour used.

Cyclohexylamine	Up to 10ppm of the amine (free or combined) in steam that may be in contact with food.
Dilauryl thiodipropionate[2]	Not over 0.01% of the fat content of the food.
Distearyl thiodipropionate[2]	Not over 0.01% of the fat content of the food.
Monoisopropyl citrate	In margarine-in amount not to exeed 0.02% by weight of the finished margarine.
Morpholine	Up to 10ppm of the amine (free or combined) in steam that may be in contact with food.
Propyl gallate[2]	Not more than 0.01% of the fat content of that food.
Resin guaiac[2]	Not over 0.1% of the fat content of the food.
Saccharin	In some special dietary foods.
Sodium diacetate	In bread: permitted in not more than 0.31 part for each 100 parts by weight of flour used.
Sodium silico-aluminate, precipitated hydrated	Satisfactory for use in salt, not more than 1%; baking powder, not more than 5%.
Sulphur dioxide (or sodium sulphite)	In molasses, dried fruits, and some other foods-200 to 300ppm (not permitted in some foods).
Thiodipropionic acid[2]	Not over 0.01% of the fat content of the food.
Tocopherol	Not more than 0.03% of the fat content of the food.

[2] Where two or more of these antioxidant are present in the same food, the total quantity of antioxident should be limited.

5.13.3 The E Numbers Classification

E100	Curcumin
E101	Riboflavin (Lactoflavin)
101(a)	Riboflavin-5'-phosphate
E102	Tartrazine
E104	Quinoline Yellow
107	Yellow 2G
E110	Sunset Yellow FCF (Orange Yellow S)
E120	Cochineal (Carmine of Cochineal or Carminic acid)
E122	Carmoisine (Azorubine)
E123	Amaranth
E124	Ponceau 4R (Cochineal Red A)
E127	Erythrosine BS
128	Red 2G
E131	Patent Blue V
E132	Indigo Carmine (Indigotine)
133	Brilliant Blue
E140	Chlorophyll
E141	Copper complexes of chlorophyll and chlorophyllins
E142	Green S (Acid Brilliant Green BS or Lissamine Green)
E150	Caramel
E151	Black PN (Brilliant Black BN)
E153	Carbon Black (Vegetable Carbon)
154	Brown FK
155	Brown HT (Chocolate Brown HT)
E160(a)	alpha-carotene, beta-carotene, gamma-carotene
E160(b)	annatto, bixin, norbixin
E160(c)	capsanthin (Capsorubin)
E160(d)	lycopene
E160(e)	beta-apo-8'-carotenal (C_{30})
E160(f)	ethyl ester of beta-apo-8'-carotenic acid (C_{30})
E161(a)	Flavoxanthin
E161(b)	Lutein
E161(c)	Cryptoxanthin
E161(d)	Rubixanthin
E161(e)	Violaxanthin
E161(f)	rhodoxanthin
E161(g)	Canthaxanthin
E162	Beetroot Red (Betanin)
E163	Anthocyanins
E170	Calcium carbonate
E171	Titanium dioxide
E172	Iron oxides, iron hydroxides
E173	Aluminium
E174	Silver
E175	Gold
E180	Pigment Rubine (Lithol Rubine BK)
E200	Sorbic acid
E201	Sodium sorbate
E202	Potassium benzoate
E203	Calcium sorbate
E210	Benzoic acid
E211	Sodium benzoate

E212	Potassium benzoate
E213	Calcium benzoate
E214	Ethyl 4-hydroxybenzoate (Ethyl *para*-hydroxybenzoate)
E215	Ethyl 4-hydroxybenzoate, sodium salt (Sodium ethyl *para*-hydroxybenzoate)
E216	Propyl 4-hydroxybenzoate (Propyl *para*-hydroxybenzoate)
E217	Propyl 4-hydroxybenzoate, sodium salt (Sodium propyl *para*-hydroxybenzoate)
E218	Methyl 4-hydroxybenzoate (Methyl *para*-hydroxybenzoate)
E219	Methyl 4-hydroxybenzoate, sodium salt (Sodium methyl *para*-hydroxybenzoate)
E220	Sulphur dioxide
E221	Sodium sulphite
E222	Sodium hydrogen sulphite (Sodium bisulphite)
E223	Sodium metabisulphite
E224	Potassium metabisulphite
E226	Calcium sulphite
E227	Calcium hydrogen sulphite (Calcium bisulphite)
E230	Biphenyl (Diphenyl)
E231	2-Hydroxybiphenyl (Orthophenylphenol)
E232	Sodium biphenyl-2-yl oxide (Sodium orthophenylphenate)
E233	2-(Thiazol-4-yl) benzimidazole (Thiabendazole)
234	Nisin
E239	Hexamine (Hexamethylenetetramine)
E249	Potassium nitrite
E250	Sodium nitrate
E251	Sodium nitrate
E252	Potassium nitrate
E260	Acetic acid
E261	Potassium acetate
E262	Sodium hydrogen diacetate
262	Sodiume acetate
E263	Calcium acetate
E270	Lactic acid
E280	Propionic acid
E281	Sodium propionate
E282	Calcium propionate
E283	Potassium propionate
E290	Carbon dioxide.
296	DL-Malic acid, L-Malic acid
297	Fumaric acid
E300	L-Ascorbic acid
E301	Sodium L-ascorbate
E302	Calcium L-ascorbate
E304	6-*O*-Palmitoyl-L-ascorbic acid (Ascorbyl palmitate)
E306	Extracts of natural origin rich in tocopherols
E307	Synthetic *alpha*-tocopherol
E308	Synthetic *gamma*-tocopherol
E309	Synthetic *delta*-tocopherol
E310	Propyl gallate
E311	Octyl gallate
E312	Dodecyl gallate
E320	Butylated hydroxyanisole (BHA)

continued over

E321	Butylated hydroxytoluene (BHT)
E322	Lecithins
E325	Sodium lactate
E326	Potassium lactate
E327	Calcium lactate
E330	Citric acid
E331	Sodium dihydrogen citrate (monoSodium citrate), diSodium citrate, triSodium citrate
E332	Potassium dihydrogen citrate (monoPotassium citrate), triPotassium citrate
E333	monoCalcium citrate, diCalcium citrate, triCalcium citrate
E334	L-(+)-Tartaric acid
E335	monoSodium L-(+)-tartrate, diSodium L-(+)-tartrate
E336	monPotassium L-(+)-tartrate (Cream of tartar), diPotassium L-(+)-tartrate
E337	Potassium sodium L-(+)-tartrate
E338	Orthophosphoric acid (Phosphoric acid)
E339	Sodium dihydrogen orthophosphate, diSodium hydrogen orthophosphate, triSodium orthophosphate
E340	Potassium dihydrogen orthophosphate, diPotassium hydrogen orthophosphate, triPotassium orthophosphate
E341	Calcium tetrahydrogen diorthophosphate, Calcium hydrogen orthophosphate, triCalcium diorthophosphate
350	Sodium malate, sodium hydrogen malate
351	Potassium malate
352	Calcium malate, calcium hydrogen malate
353	Metatartaric acid
355	Adipic acid
363	Succinic acid
370	1,4-Heptonolactone
375	Nicotinic acid
380	triAmmonium citrate
381	Ammonium ferric citrate
385	Calcium disodium ethylenendiamine-NNN'N' tetra-acetate (Calcium disodium EDTA)
E400	Alginic acid
E401	Sodium alginate
E402	Potassium alginate
E403	Ammonium alginate
E404	Calcium alginate
E405	Propane-1,2,-diol alginate (Propylene glycol alginate)
E406	Agar
E407	Carrageenan
E410	Locust bean gum (Carob gum)
E412	Guar Gum
E413	Tragacanth
E414	Gum arabic (Acacia)
E415	Xanthan gum
416	Karaya gum
E420	Sorbitol, sorbitol syrup
E421	Mannitol
E422	Glycerol
430	Polyoxyethylene (8) stearate
431	Polyoxyethylene (40) stearate
432	Polyoxyethylene (20) sorbitan monolaurate (Polysorbate 20)
433	Polyoxyethylene (20) sorbitan mono-oleate (Polysorbate 80)

434	Polyoxyethylene (20) sorbitan monopalmitate (Polysorbate 40)
435	Polyoxyethylene (20) sorbitan monostearate (Polysorbate 60)
436	Polyoxyethylene (20) sorbitan tristearate (Polysorbate 65)
E440(a)	Pectin
E440(b)	Amidated pectin
442	Ammonium phosphatides
E450(a)	*di*Sodium dihydrogen diphosphate, *tri*Sodium diphosphate, *tetra*Sodium diphosphate, *tetra*Potassium diphosphate
E450(b)	*penta*Sodium triphosphate, *penta*Potassium triphosphate
E450(c)	Sodium polyphosphates, Potassium polyphosphates
E460	Microcrystalline cellulose, *Alpha*-cellulose (Powdered cellulose)
E461	Methylcellulose
E463	Hydroxypropylcellulose
E464	Hydroxypropylmethylcellulose
E465	Ethylmethylcellulose
E466	Carboxymethylcellulose, sodium salt (CMC)
E470	Sodium, potassium and calcium salts of fatty acids
E471	Mono- and di-glycerides of fatty acids
E472(a)	Acetic acid esters of mono- and di-glycerides of fatty acids
E472(b)	Lactic acid esters of mono- and di-glycerides of fatty acids (Lactoglycerides)
E473	Sucrose esters of fattt acids
E474	Sucroglycerides
E475	Polyglycerol esters of fatty acids
476	Polyglycerol esters of polycondensed fatty acids of caster oil (Polyglycerol polyricinoleate)
E477	Propane-1,2-diol esters of fatty acids
478	Lactylated fatty acid esters of glycerol and propane-1,2-diol
E481	Sodium stearoyl-2-lactylate
E482	Calcium stearoyl-2-lactylate
E483	Stearyl tartrate
491	Sorbitan monostearate
492	Sorbitan tristearate
493	Sorbitan monolaurate
494	Sorbitan mono-oleate
495	Sorbitan monopalmitate
500	Sodium carbonate, Sodium hydrogen carbonate (Bicarbonate of soda), Sodium sesquicarbonate
501	Potassium carbonate, Potassium hydrogen carbonate
503	Ammonium carbonate, Ammonium hydrogen carbonate
504	Magnesium carbonate
507	Hydrochloric acid
508	Potasium chloride
509	Calcium chloride
510	Ammonium chloride
513	Sulphuric acid
514	Sodium sulphate
515	Potassium sulphate
516	Calcium sulphate
518	Magnesium sulphate
524	Sodium hydroxide
525	Potassium hydroxide
526	Calcium hydroxide
527	Ammonium hydroxide

continued over

528	Magnesium hydroxide
529	Calcium oxide
530	Magnesium oxide
535	Sodium ferrocyanide (Sodium hexacyanoferrate (II))
536	Potassium ferrocyanide (Potassium hexacyanoferrate (II))
540	*di*Calcium diphosphate
541	Sodium aluminium phosphate
542	Edible bone phosphate
544	Calcium polyphosphates
545	Ammonium polyphosphates
551	Silicon dioxide (Silica)
552	Calcium silicate
553(a)	Magnesium silicate synthetic, Magnesium trisilicate
553(b)	Talc
554	Aluminium sodium silicate
556	Aluminium calcium silicate
558	Bentonite
559	Kaolin
570	Stearic acid
572	Magnesium stearate
575	D–Glucono–1,5–lactone (Glucono *delta*–lactone)
576	Sodium gluconate
577	Potassium gluconate
578	Calcium gluconate
620	L–glutamic acid
621	Sodium hydrogen L–glutamate (*mono*Sodium glutamate or MSG)
622	Potassium hydrogen L–glutamate (*mono*Potassium glutamate)
623	Calcium dihydrogen di–L–glutamate (Calcium glutamate)
627	Guanosine 5'–(disodium phosphate) (Sodium guanylate)
631	Inosine 5'–(disodium phosphate) (Sodium inosinate)
635	Sodium 5'–ribonucleotide
636	Maltol
637	Ethyl maltol
900	Dimethylpolysiloxane

5.14 Recommended Storage Conditions

5.14.1 Frozen Food Storage Data

Maximum Home-Storage Periods to Maintain Good Quality in Purchased Frozen Foods

Food	Approx. Holding Time @ 0°F Months	Food	Approx. Holding Time @ 0°F Months
FRUIT		**COOKED MEATS**	
Cherries, peaches, rasberries, strawberries	12	Meat dinners, meat pie, Swiss steak	3
Fruit juice concentrates (apple, grape, orange)	12	**POULTRY**	
		Chicken (cut up)	9
BAKED GOODS		Livers	3
White bread	3	Whole	12
Cinnamon rolls	2	Duck (whole)	6
Plain rolls	3	Goose (whole)	6
		Turkey (cut up)	6
CAKES		Whole	12
Angel	2	Cooked Chicken/Turkey slices in gravy	6
Chiffon	2	Chicken/Turkey pies	6
Chocolate layer	4	Fried chicken	4
Fruit	12		
Pound	6	**FISH**	
Yellow	6	Fillets (cod, flounder, haddock, halibut, pollack)	6
Danish pastry	3	Mullet, perch, trout, bass	2-3
Doughnuts	3	Salmon steaks	2
Pies (unbaked)	8	Sea trout	3
		Whiting (drawn)	4
BEEF			
Hamburger steaks	4	**SHELLFISH**	
Roasts	12	Clams	3
Steaks	12	Crabmeat	3-10
		Oysters	4
LAMB		Shrimps	12
Patties (ground meat)	4	Cooked fish and shellfish	3
Roasts	9		
		FROZEN DESSERTS	
PORK		Ice cream	1
Cured	2	Sherbert	1
Fresh, chops	4		
Fresh, roasts	8	**VEGETABLES**	
Fresh, sausage	2	Asparagus, beans, corn, peas, cauliflower, spinach	8
VEAL			
Cutlets, chops, roasts	9		

Source: Handbook for the Home. 1973. Yearbook of Agriculture. USDA.

Approximate Storage Life of Frozen Foods at Various Temperatures

Food Type	+10°F Months	0°F Months	−10°F Months
FISH			
Fish, fatty	4	6-8	10-12
Fish, lean	6	10-12	14-16
FRUIT			
Apricots, with ascorbic acid	6-8	18-24	24
Apricots, without ascorbic acid	3-4	8-10	12-14
Peaches, with ascorbic acid	6-8	18-24	24
Peaches, without ascorbic acid	3-4	8-10	12-14
Rasberries, sugared	8-10	18	24
Rasberries, without sugar/syrup	6-8	12	18
Strawberries, sliced	8-10	18	24
MEATS			
Beef, roasts	6-8	16-18	18-24
Lamb	5-7	14-16	16-18
Pork, roasts	4	8-10	12-15
Pork, sausage	2	4-6	8-10
POULTRY			
Poultry giblets	1	3-5	8-10
Poultry, roasting	4	8-10	12-15
SHELLFISH			
Lobsters	3-4	8-10	10-12
Shrimp, raw	6	12	16-18
VEGETABLES			
Asparagus	4-6	8-12	16-18
Beans, snap	4-6	8-12	16-18
Beans, lima	6-8	14-16	24+
Broccoli	6-8	14-16	24+
Brussels sprouts	4-6	8-12	16-18
Cauliflower	6-8	14-16	24+
Corn on the cob	4-6	8-10	12-14
Corn, cut	12	24	36+
Carrots	12	24	36+
Mushrooms	3-4	8-10	12-14
Peas	6-8	14-16	24+
Pumpkin	12	24	36+
Spinach	6-8	14-16	24+
Squash	12	24	36+

Source: Tressler D K and Evers C F, The Freezing Preservation of Foods, 3rd Edition Vol 1, AVI Publishing Co, Westport Comm.

5.14.2 Frozen Meat Storage Data

Recommended Length of Storage for Frozen Meats

Meat	Maximum Number of Months 0°F
Beef	
Roast, steaks	6-12
Ground	2-3
Veal	
Roasts	4-8
Cutlets, chops	3-4
Ground meat	2-3
Pork	
Roasts	4-6
Chops	3-4
Sausage, without salt	1-2
Ham, cured	1-2
Bacon	less than 1
Poultry	6-12

Source: Simonds L A and Vanstavern B D 1975, Buying Meat for Locker or Home Freezer, Ohio Univ, Coop, Ext, Serv.

5.14.3 Modified Atmosphere Storage

When deciding upon a modified atmosphere (gas) packaging as a method of preserving chilled foods and extending the shelf life, it is essential to get the mix of 'gas cocktail' right. Five of the eight main spoilage mechanisms may be prevented or retarded by use of different modified atmospheres. Choice of atmosphere depends of course, on type of food product handled.

Spoilage Mechanisms

Ageing, staling and ultraviolet light spoilage	: no gas protection
Oxidation (including rancidity, hazes, off flavours)	: N_2
Bacterial Growth	: CO_2, N_2O
Enzymic action	: CO, N_2O, $(CH_2)_2O$
Mould growth	: N_2 or CO_2
Insect attack	: N_2 or CO_2

The Effect of Trace Gases on the Spoilage Mechanisms

Carbon Monoxide (CO)	Stabilises blood pigments. Suppresses autolytic enzymes.
Nitrous Oxide (N_2O)	Dry blanch for fruit and vegetables. Prevents oxidation, rancidity and bacterial attack.
Ethylene Oxide $(CH_2)_2O$	Sterilant, marked preservative action. Not recommended for products containing salt.
Sulphur Dioxide (SO_2)	Sterilant, powerful preservative bleaches, destroys thiamin.

Functions of Gases in Modified Atmosphere Storage

Oxygen

Sustains basic metabolism. Prevents anaerobic spoilage.

Nitrogen

Chemically inert. Prevents oxidation rancidity, mould growth and insect attack.

Carbon Dioxide

Inhibits bacterial and mould activity. Fat soluble. High concentrations can injure product. Not suitable for dairy products.

Recommended Gas Mixtures for Food Commodities

For the full benefits of modified atmosphere packaging to be obtained it is essential that good hygiene practices be followed, and rapid chilling with accurate temperature control is recommended.

Precise gas mixtures may vary from those given below for specific food products. Ethylene oxide and Carbon monoxide are not approved food additives.

In all cases the balance of the mixture (or the only gas in the case of hard cheese, bakery products with dairy fillings, and pasta) is nitrogen.

Commodity	Oxygen %	Carbon Dioxide %	Trace Gas %
Red Meat	50 plus	15-25	–
Fish, white	–	40	–
Fish, oily	–	20	–
Fish, pigmented	5	30	1 CO
Poultry	–	25	–
Green leaf vegetables	less than 5	2	1 CO
Cauliflower, etc	7	10	–
Mushrooms	7	–	5 N_2O
Citrus fruit	2.5	10	1 CO
Navel oranges	5	5	1 CO
Strawberries	2.5	15	–
Tomatoes	4	4	–
Apples	1.5-2.5	nil to 1	–
Pears	2	10	–
Cheese, hard	–	–	–
Cheese, active	–	20 OR	20 N_2O
Bakery, non dairy	–	100	–
Bakery, dairy	–	–	–
Pasta	–	–	–

Index

174